GRAPHIC BIOGRAPHIES

Helen Keller
COURAGEOUS ADVOCATE

by Scott R. Welvaert
illustrated by Cynthia Martin
and Keith Tucker

Consultant:

Keller Johnson Thompson

Vice President of Education

The Helen Keller Foundation

Capstone
press

Mankato, Minnesota

Graphic Library is published by Capstone Press,
151 Good Counsel Drive, P.O. Box 669, Mankato, Minnesota 56002.
www.capstonepress.com

Printed in the United States of America

1 2 3 4 5 6 10 09 08 07 06 05

Library of Congress Cataloging-in-Publication Data
Welvaert, Scott R.
Helen Keller : courageous advocate / written by Scott R. Welvaert; illustrated by Cynthia Martin and Keith Tucker.
p. cm.—(Graphic library. Graphic biographies)
Includes bibliographical references and index.
ISBN 0-7368-4964-5 (hardcover)
1. Keller, Helen, 1880–1968—Juvenile literature. 2. Blind-deaf women—United States—Biography—Juvenile literature. I. Cynthia Martin and Keith Tucker, ill. II. Title. III. Series.
HV1624.K4.W43 2006
362.4'1'092—dc22 2005006463

Summary: Describes in graphic format the life of Helen Keller, a blind and deaf woman, who became an author and advocate for the blind.

Art and Editorial Direction
Jason Knudson and Blake A. Hoena

Designers
Jason Knudson and Jennifer Bergstrom

Editor
Erika L. Shores

Editor's note: Direct quotations from primary sources are indicated by a yellow background.

Direct quotations appear on the following pages:
Page 9, from *Helen and Teacher: The Story of Helen Keller and Anne Sullivan Macy* by Joseph P. Lash. (New York: Delacorte Press/Seymour Lawrence, 1980).
Pages 19, 22, 24, from *The Story of My Life*, by Helen Keller (New York: Doubleday, Page and Company, 1903).
Page 23, from *The World I Live In* by Helen Keller (New York: The Century Co., 1908).
Page 27, from the Royal National Institute of the Blind,
(http://www.rnib.org.uk/xpedio/groups/public/documents/publicwebsite/public_keller.hcsp#P119_15629)

Table of Contents

CHAPTER 1

Silence and Darkness 4

CHAPTER 2

A Miracle 10

CHAPTER 3

Going to School 16

CHAPTER 4

Working for Others 24

More about Helen Keller 28

Glossary 30

Internet Sites 30

Read More 31

Bibliography 31

Index 32

CHAPTER 1

Silence and Darkness

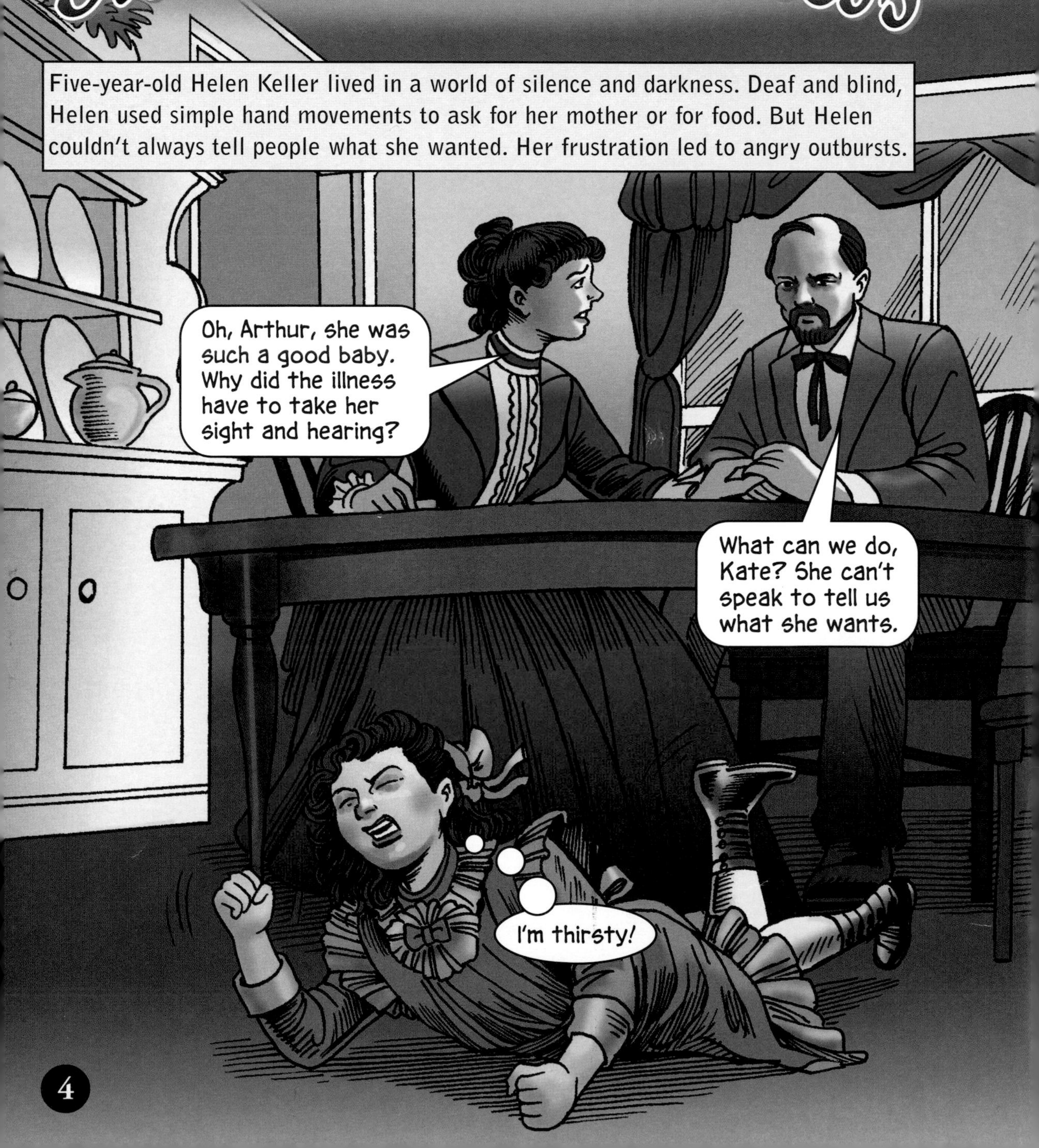

Five-year-old Helen Keller lived in a world of silence and darkness. Deaf and blind, Helen used simple hand movements to ask for her mother or for food. But Helen couldn't always tell people what she wanted. Her frustration led to angry outbursts.
Oh, Arthur, she was such a good baby. Why did the illness have to take her sight and hearing?
What can we do, Kate? She can't speak to tell us what she wants.
I'm thirsty!

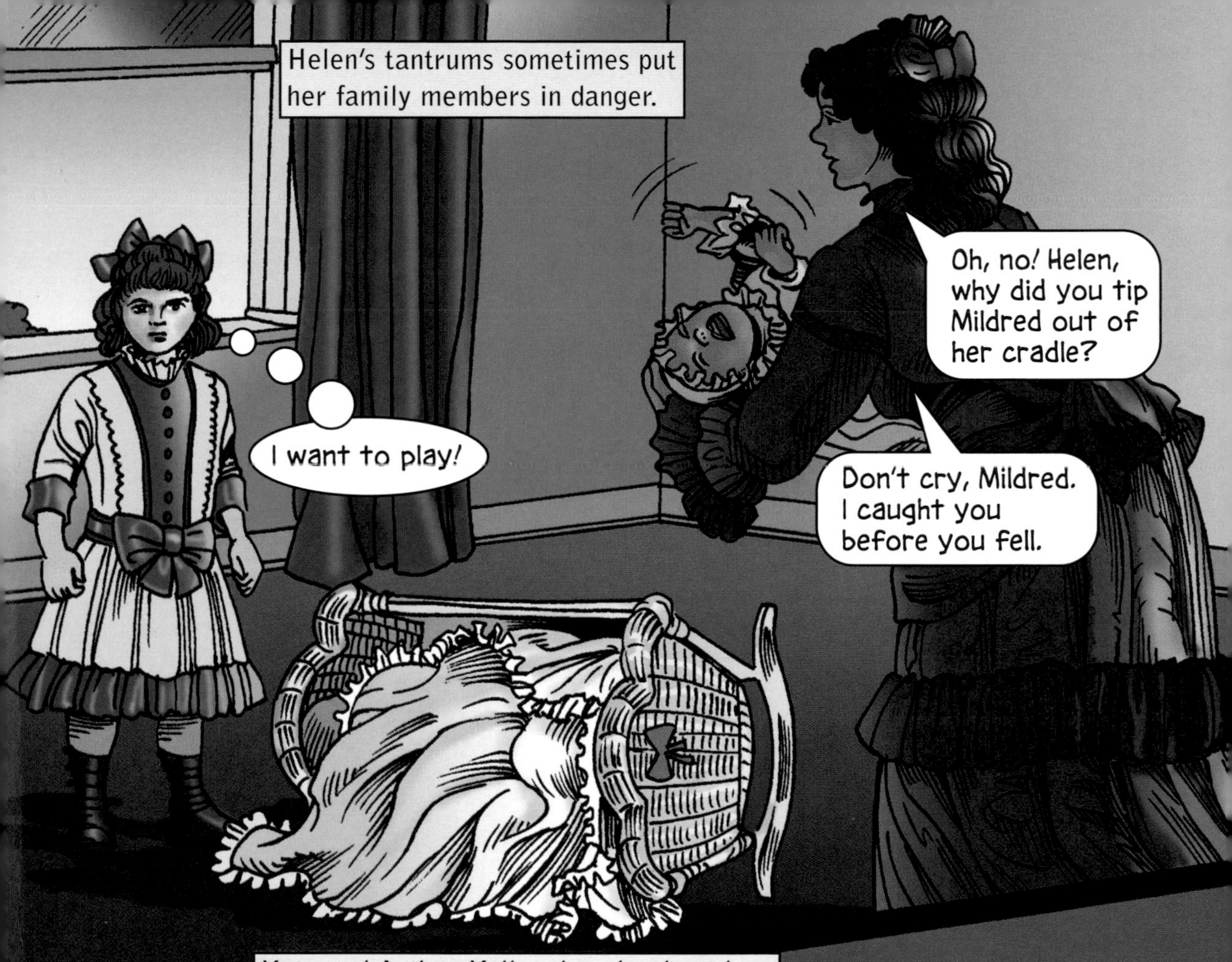
Helen's tantrums sometimes put her family members in danger.
I want to play!
Oh, no! Helen, why did you tip Mildred out of her cradle?
Don't cry, Mildred. I caught you before you fell.

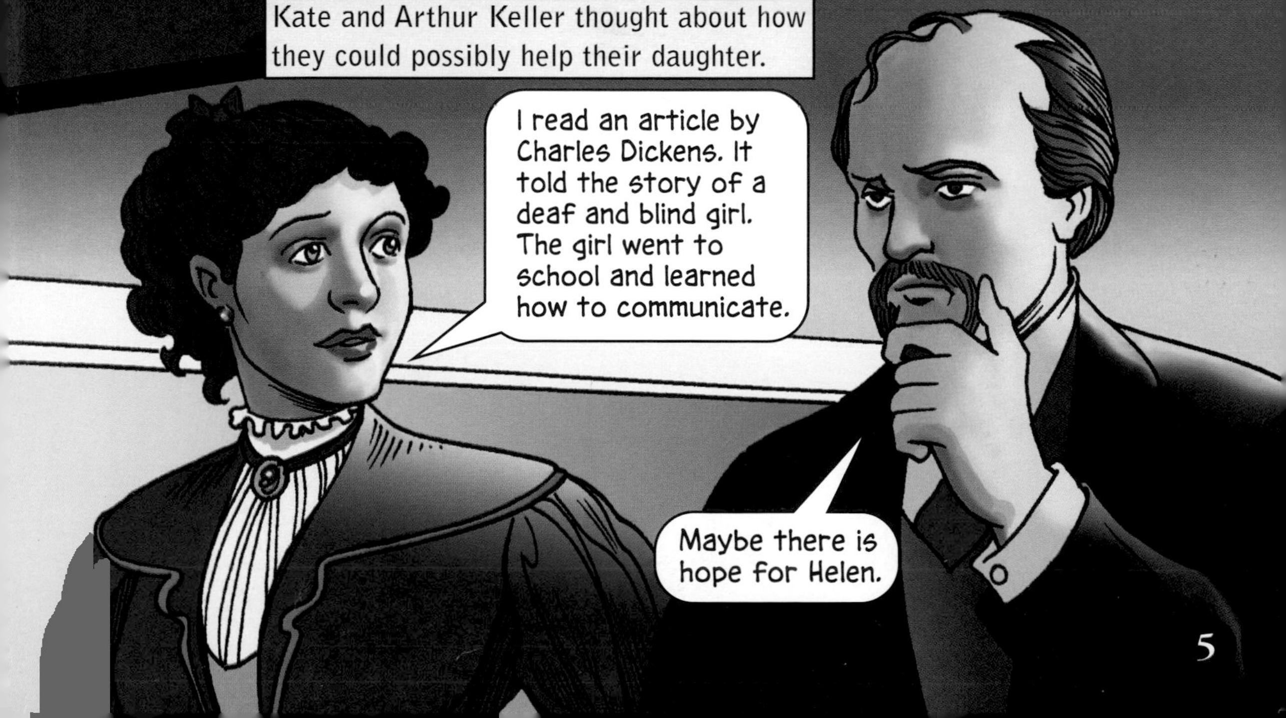
Kate and Arthur Keller thought about how they could possibly help their daughter.
I read an article by Charles Dickens. It told the story of a deaf and blind girl. The girl went to school and learned how to communicate.
Maybe there is hope for Helen.

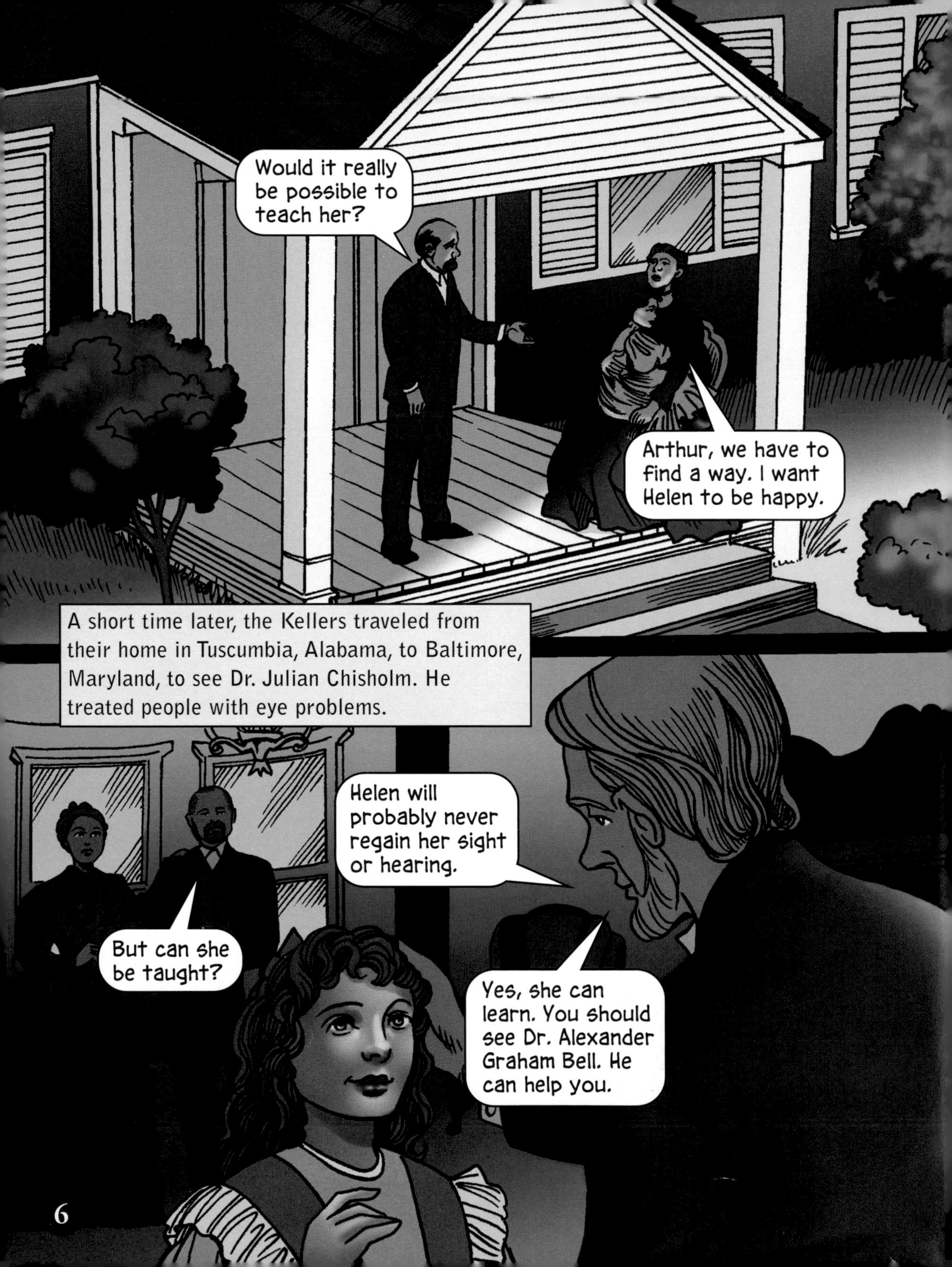
Would it really be possible to teach her?
Arthur, we have to find a way. I want Helen to be happy.
A short time later, the Kellers traveled from their home in Tuscumbia, Alabama, to Baltimore, Maryland, to see Dr. Julian Chisholm. He treated people with eye problems.
But can she be taught?
Helen will probably never regain her sight or hearing.
Yes, she can learn. You should see Dr. Alexander Graham Bell. He can help you.

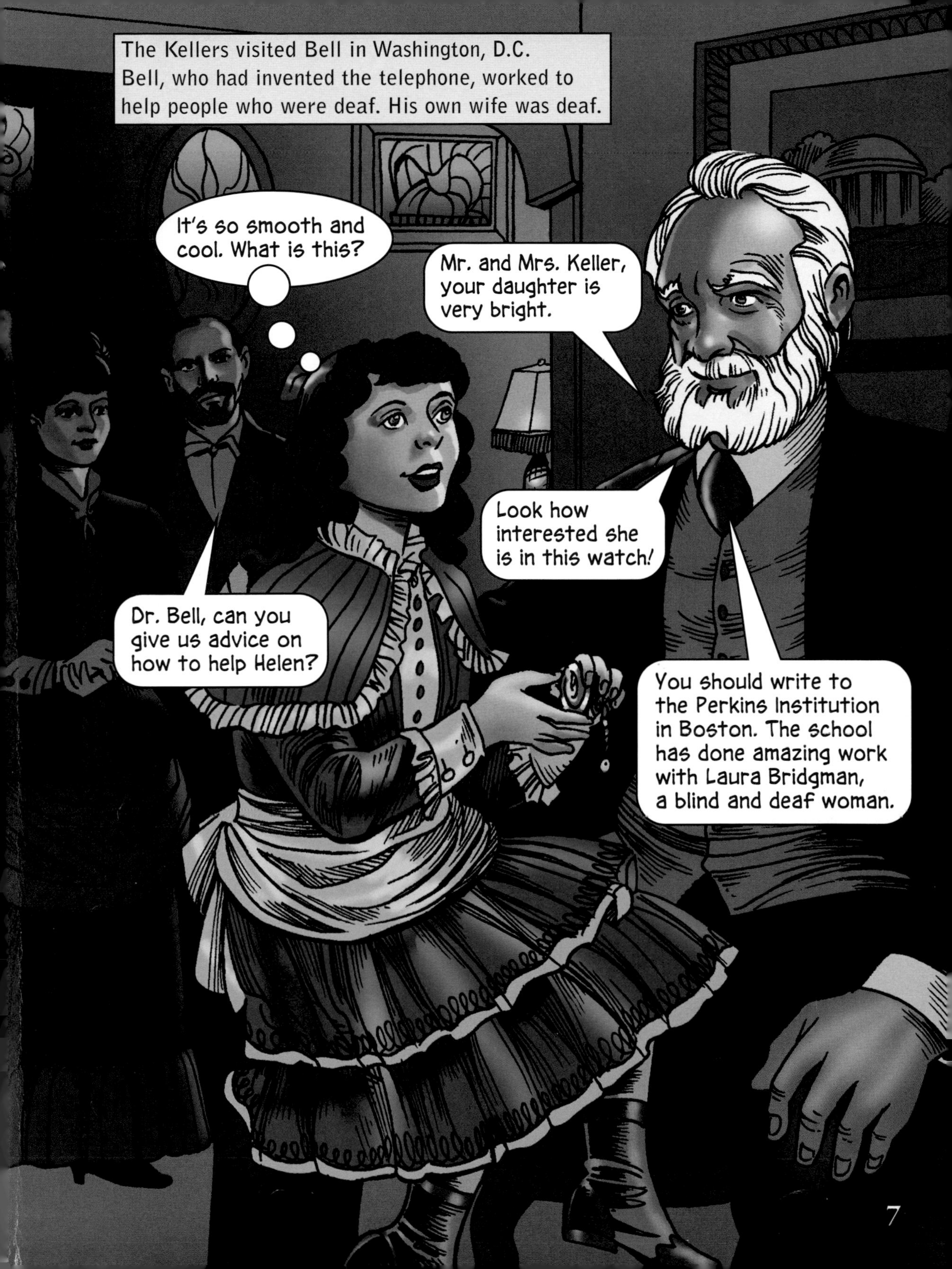
The Kellers visited Bell in Washington, D.C. Bell, who had invented the telephone, worked to help people who were deaf. His own wife was deaf.
It's so smooth and cool. What is this?
Mr. and Mrs. Keller, your daughter is very bright.
Look how interested she is in this watch!
Dr. Bell, can you give us advice on how to help Helen?
You should write to the Perkins Institution in Boston. The school has done amazing work with Laura Bridgman, a blind and deaf woman.

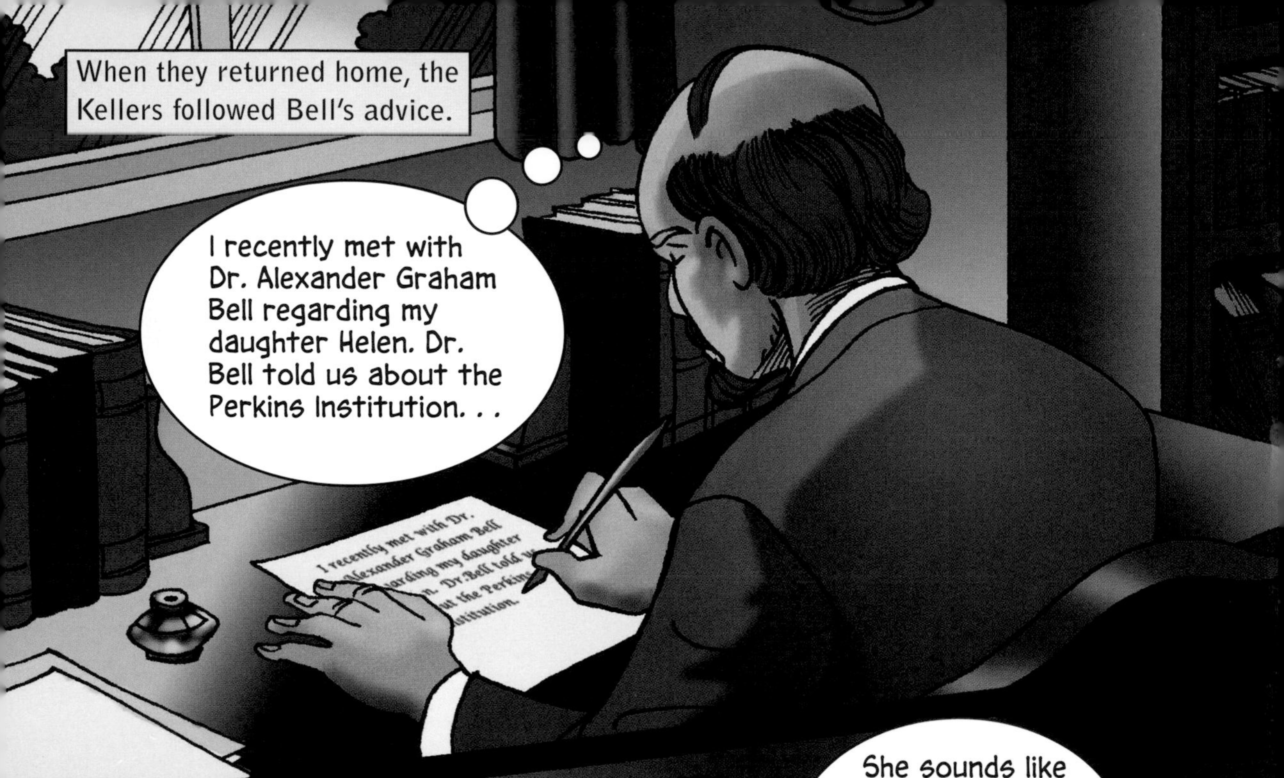
When they returned home, the Kellers followed Bell's advice.
I recently met with Dr. Alexander Graham Bell regarding my daughter Helen. Dr. Bell told us about the Perkins Institution. . .

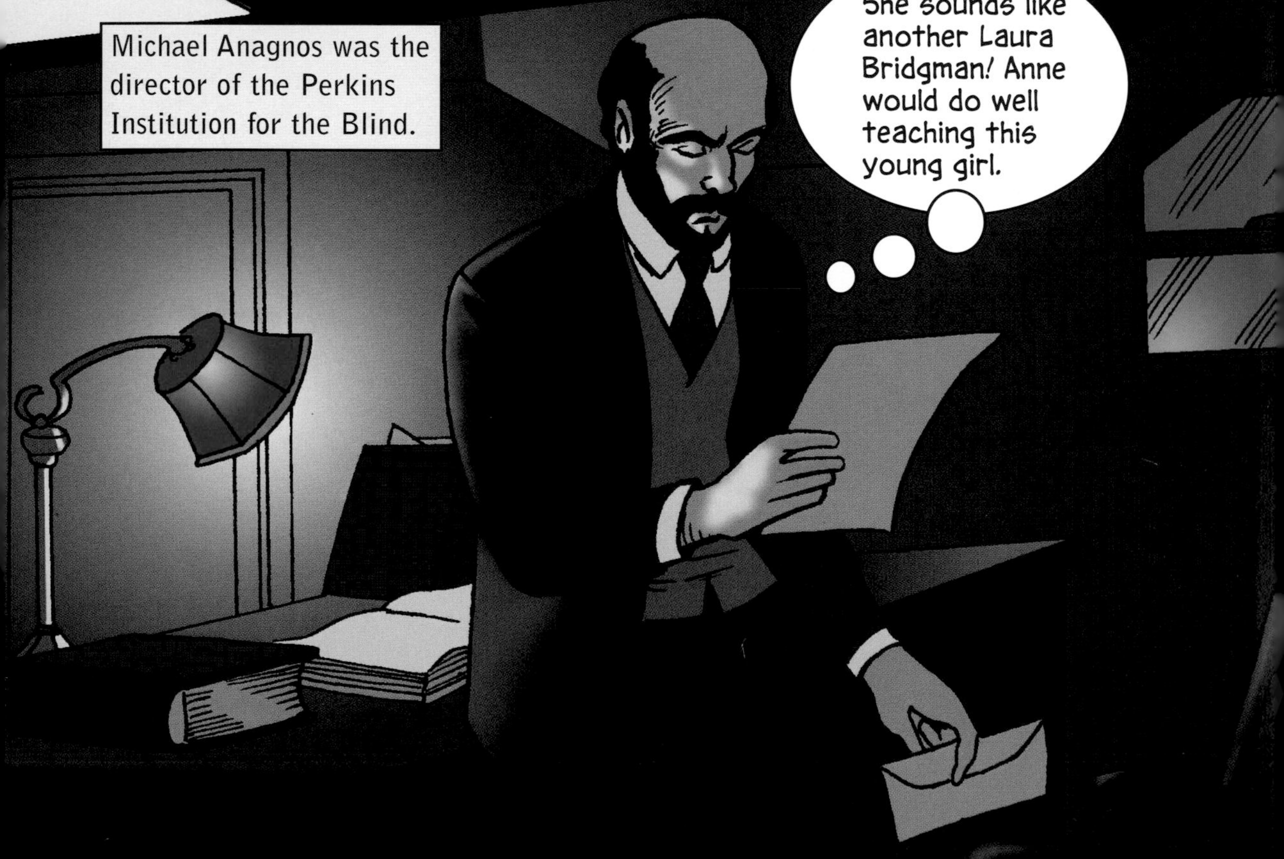
Michael Anagnos was the director of the Perkins Institution for the Blind.
She sounds like another Laura Bridgman! Anne would do well teaching this young girl.

Twenty-one-year-old Anne Sullivan was a recent graduate from Perkins. An orphan, Anne was nearly blind when she came to the school. After many operations, Anne's eyesight had improved.
Do I know enough to teach this little girl?
If anyone can teach her, it's you. Anne, I'm confident you'll succeed.
In 1887, the Kellers received a letter from Anagnos.
What does he say?
I have reason to believe that Miss Sullivan will make a wonderful teacher and most excellent companion for your little daughter.

CHAPTER 2

A Miracle

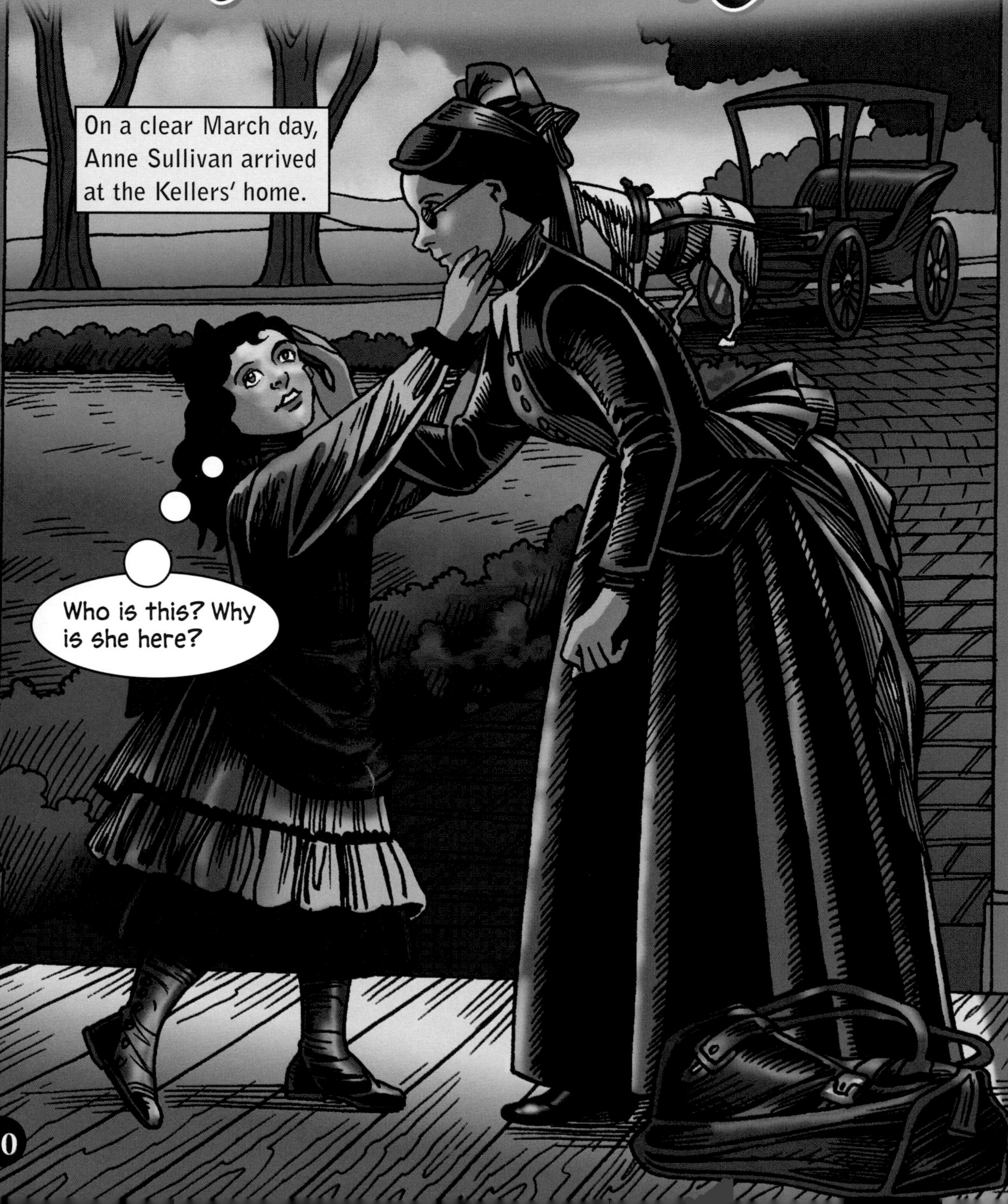
On a clear March day, Anne Sullivan arrived at the Kellers' home.
Who is this? Why is she here?

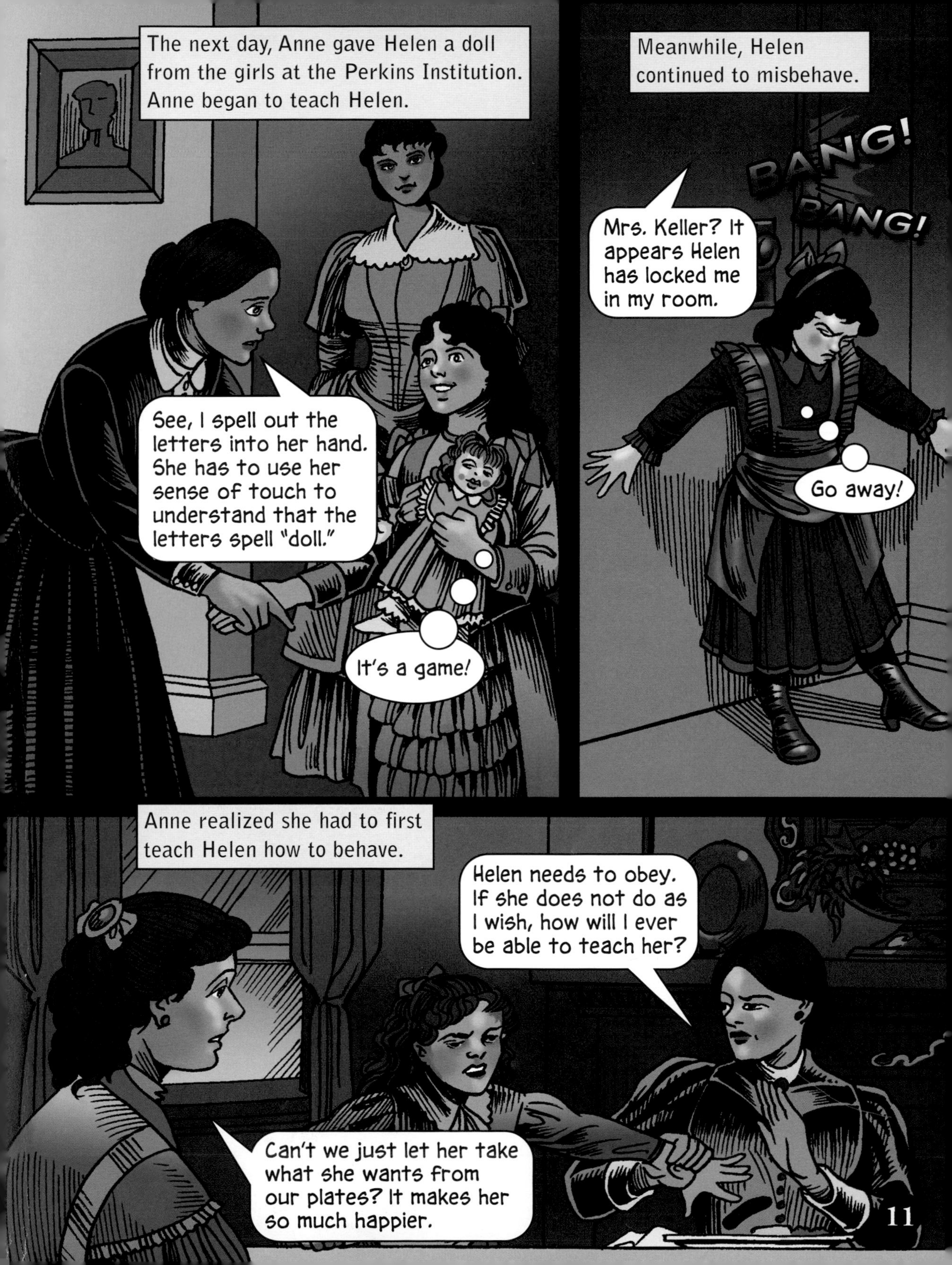

The next day, Anne gave Helen a doll from the girls at the Perkins Institution. Anne began to teach Helen.
See, I spell out the letters into her hand. She has to use her sense of touch to understand that the letters spell "doll."
It's a game!
Meanwhile, Helen continued to misbehave.
BANG! BANG!
Mrs. Keller? It appears Helen has locked me in my room.
Go away!
Anne realized she had to first teach Helen how to behave.
Helen needs to obey. If she does not do as I wish, how will I ever be able to teach her?
Can't we just let her take what she wants from our plates? It makes her so much happier.

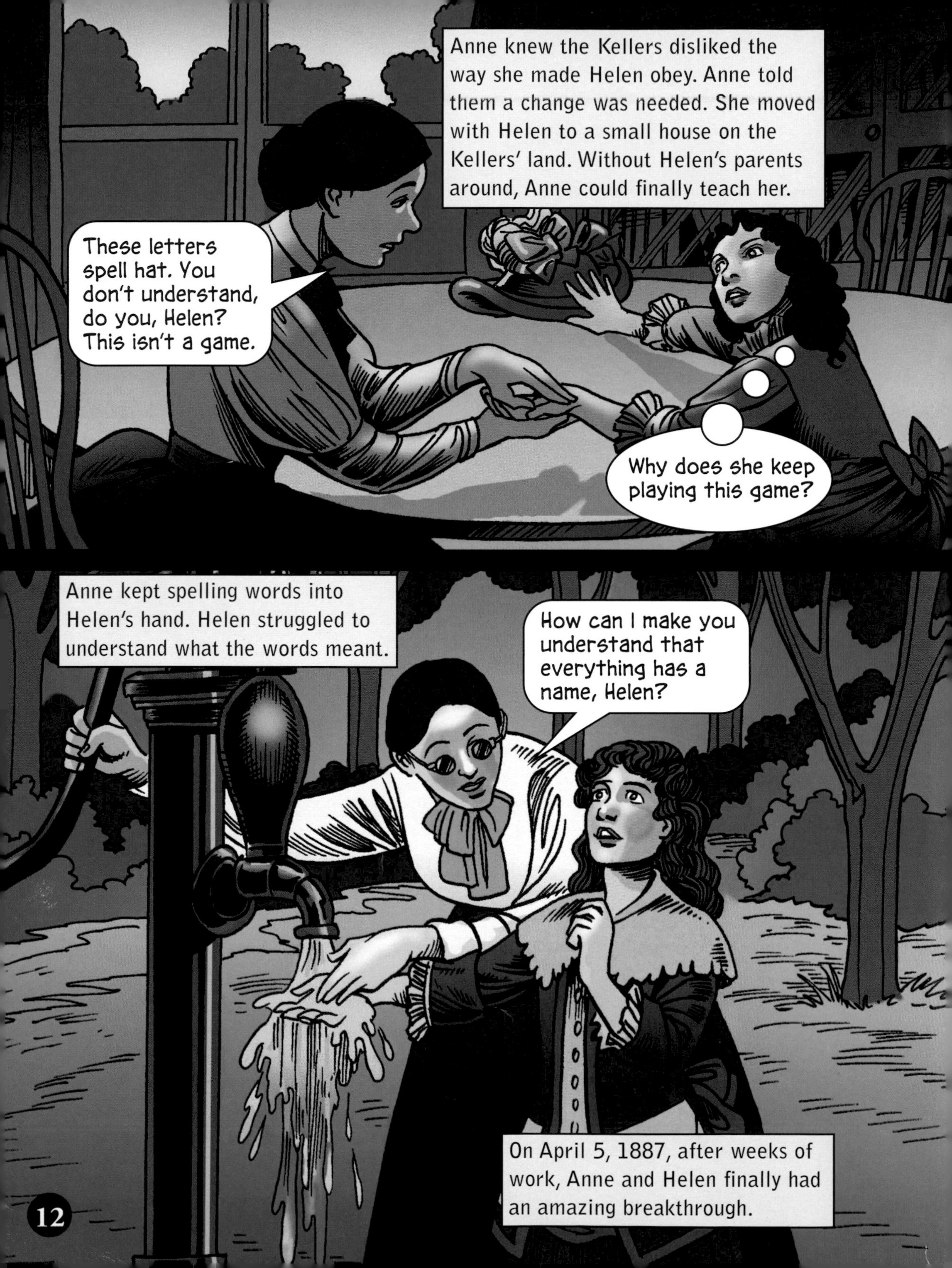
Anne knew the Kellers disliked the way she made Helen obey. Anne told them a change was needed. She moved with Helen to a small house on the Kellers' land. Without Helen's parents around, Anne could finally teach her.
These letters spell hat. You don't understand, do you, Helen? This isn't a game.
Why does she keep playing this game?
Anne kept spelling words into Helen's hand. Helen struggled to understand what the words meant.
How can I make you understand that everything has a name, Helen?
On April 5, 1887, after weeks of work, Anne and Helen finally had an amazing breakthrough.

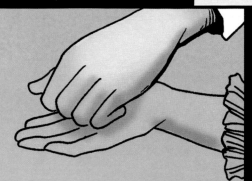

As they stood before the water pump, Anne had an idea. She spelled W-A-T-E-R into Helen's hand, while running water flowed over her other hand.

Water! Her hand signals mean water!

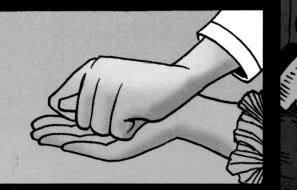

That's right! Water. The letters stand for water.

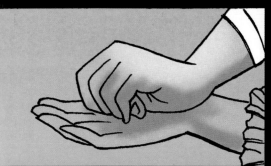

It was a miracle. When Helen spelled the word back to Anne, Anne knew Helen understood W-A-T-E-R stood for the cool something flowing over her hand.

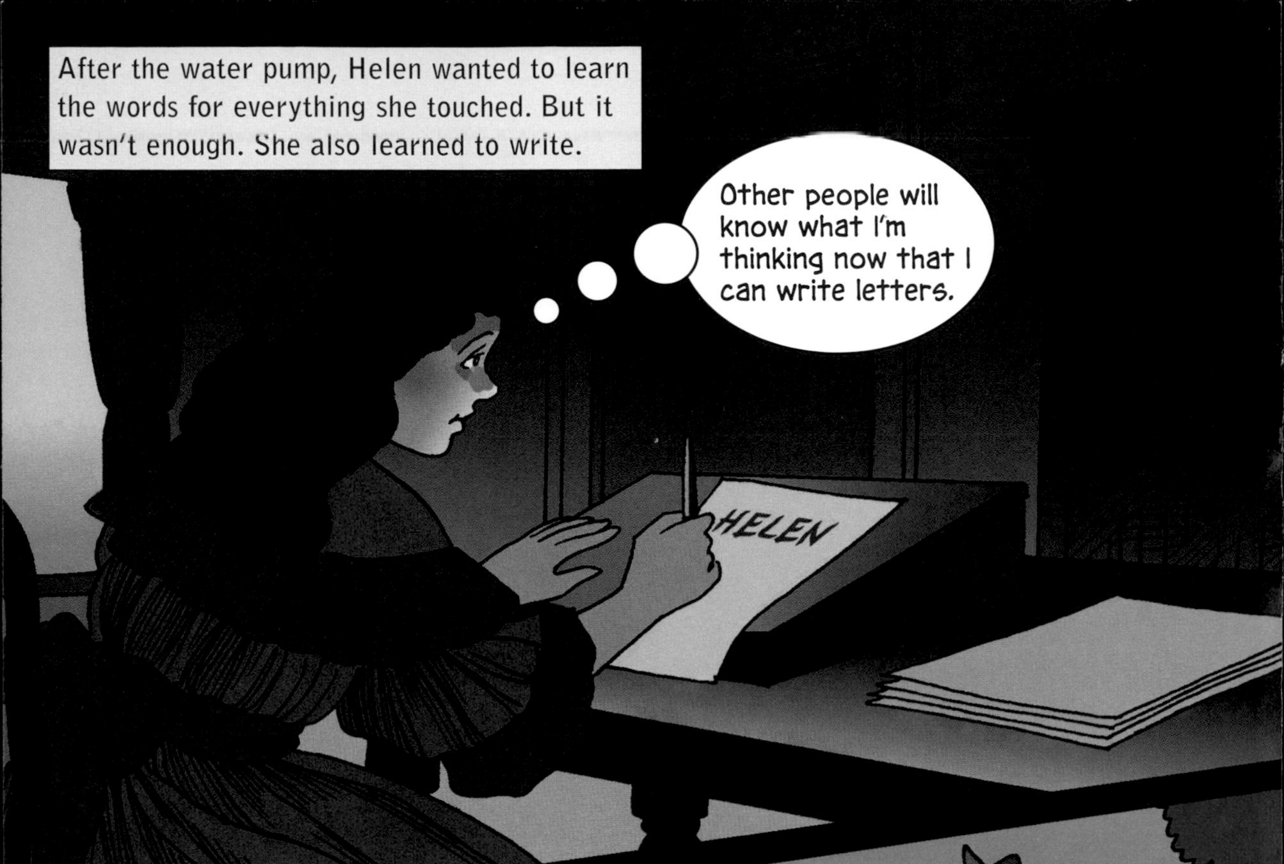
After the water pump, Helen wanted to learn the words for everything she touched. But it wasn't enough. She also learned to write.
Other people will know what I'm thinking now that I can write letters.
HELEN

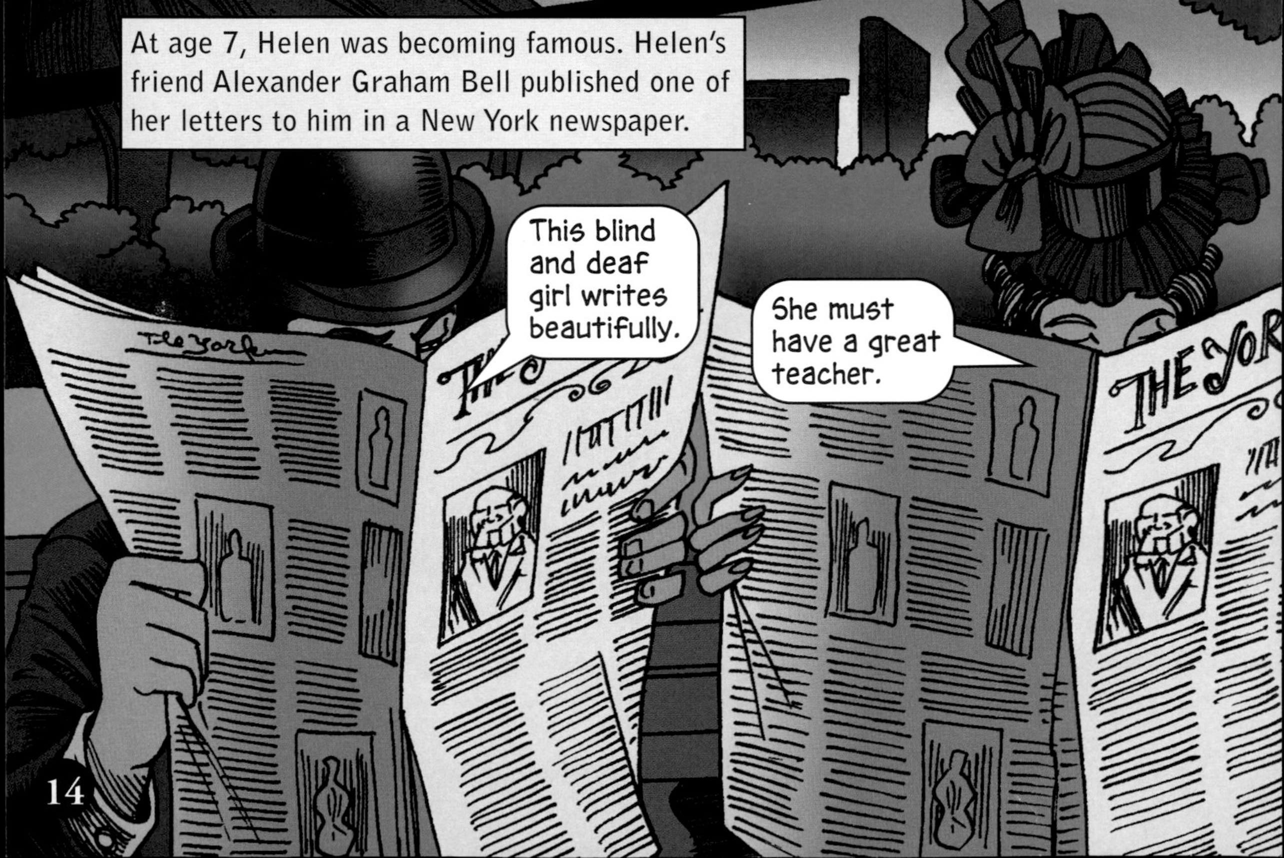
At age 7, Helen was becoming famous. Helen's friend Alexander Graham Bell published one of her letters to him in a New York newspaper.
This blind and deaf girl writes beautifully.
She must have a great teacher.
THE YORK

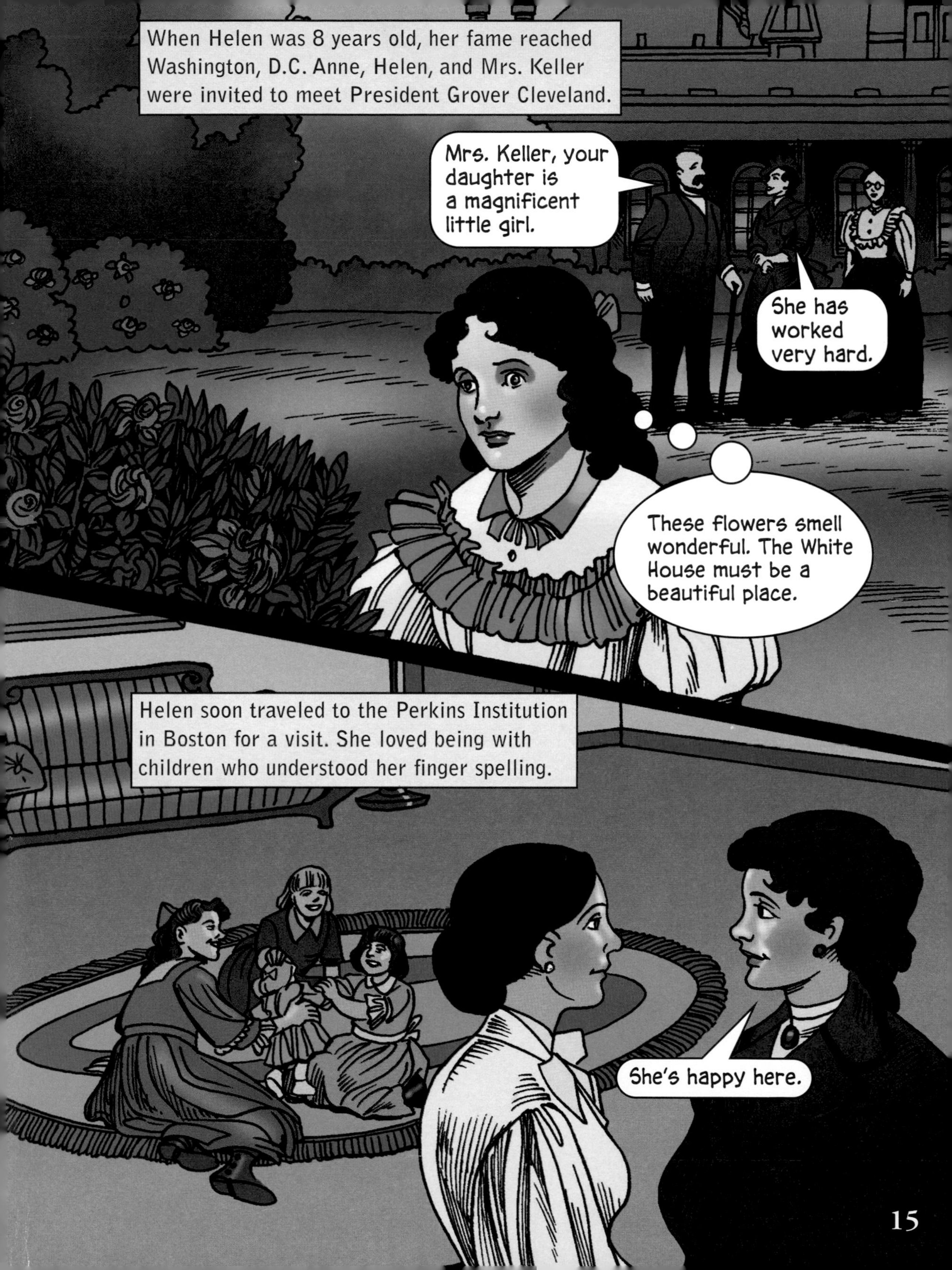
When Helen was 8 years old, her fame reached Washington, D.C. Anne, Helen, and Mrs. Keller were invited to meet President Grover Cleveland.
Mrs. Keller, your daughter is a magnificent little girl.
She has worked very hard.
These flowers smell wonderful. The White House must be a beautiful place.
Helen soon traveled to the Perkins Institution in Boston for a visit. She loved being with children who understood her finger spelling.
She's happy here.

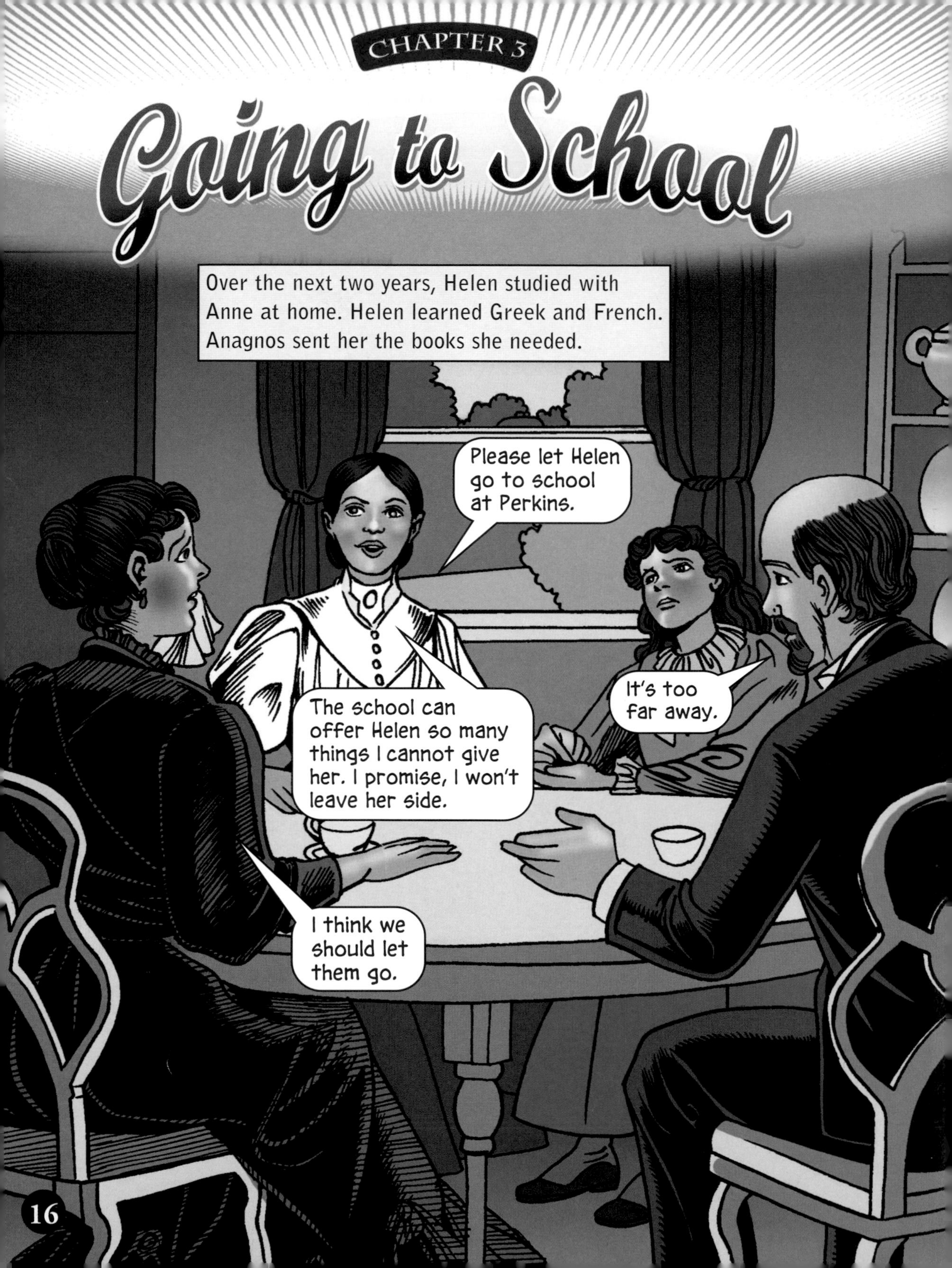

CHAPTER 3
Going to School
Over the next two years, Helen studied with Anne at home. Helen learned Greek and French. Anagnos sent her the books she needed.
Please let Helen go to school at Perkins.
The school can offer Helen so many things I cannot give her. I promise, I won't leave her side.
It's too far away.
I think we should let them go.

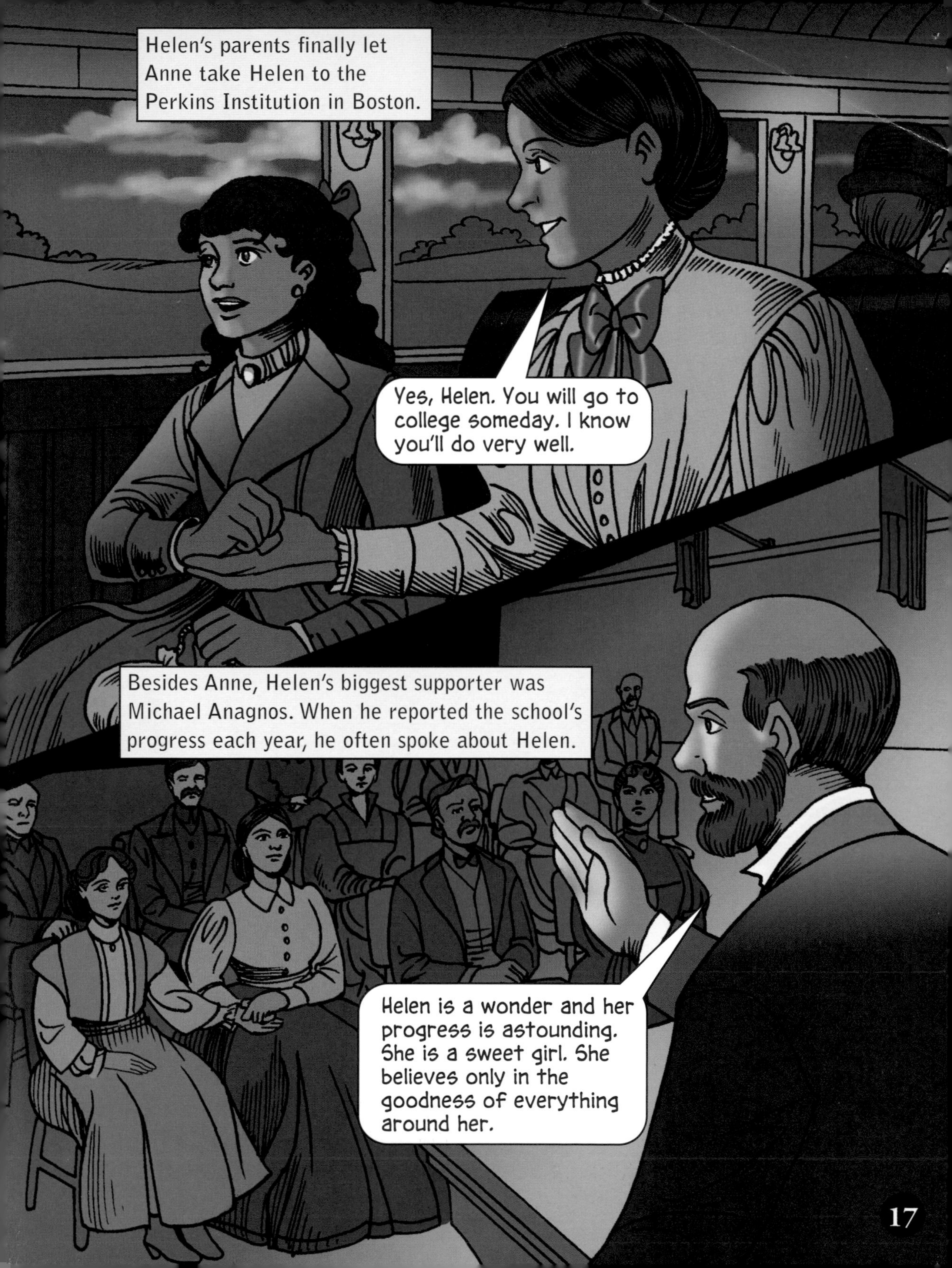
Helen's parents finally let Anne take Helen to the Perkins Institution in Boston.
Yes, Helen. You will go to college someday. I know you'll do very well.
Besides Anne, Helen's biggest supporter was Michael Anagnos. When he reported the school's progress each year, he often spoke about Helen.
Helen is a wonder and her progress is astounding. She is a sweet girl. She believes only in the goodness of everything around her.

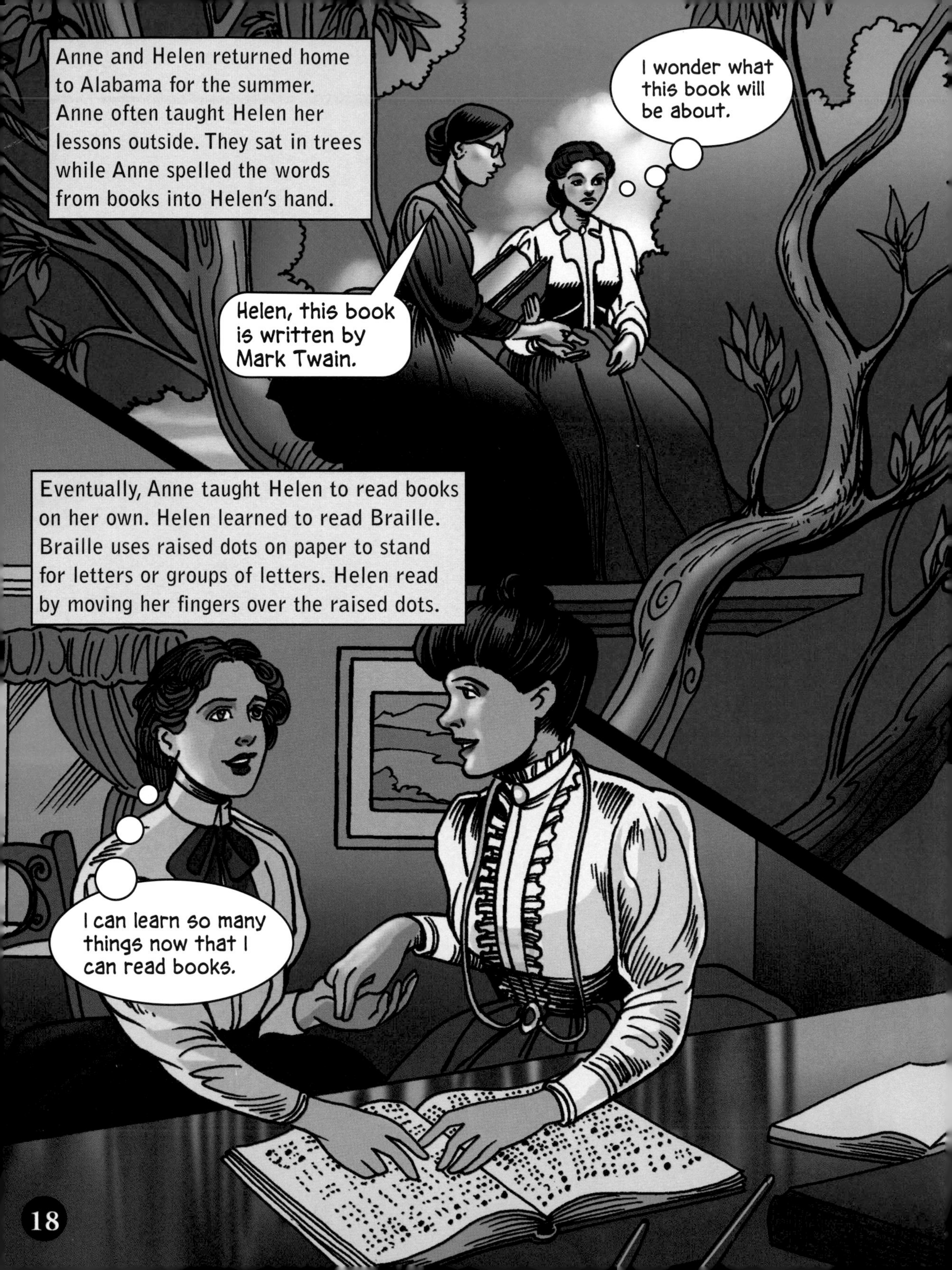
Anne and Helen returned home to Alabama for the summer. Anne often taught Helen her lessons outside. They sat in trees while Anne spelled the words from books into Helen's hand.
I wonder what this book will be about.
Helen, this book is written by Mark Twain.
Eventually, Anne taught Helen to read books on her own. Helen learned to read Braille. Braille uses raised dots on paper to stand for letters or groups of letters. Helen read by moving her fingers over the raised dots.
I can learn so many things now that I can read books.

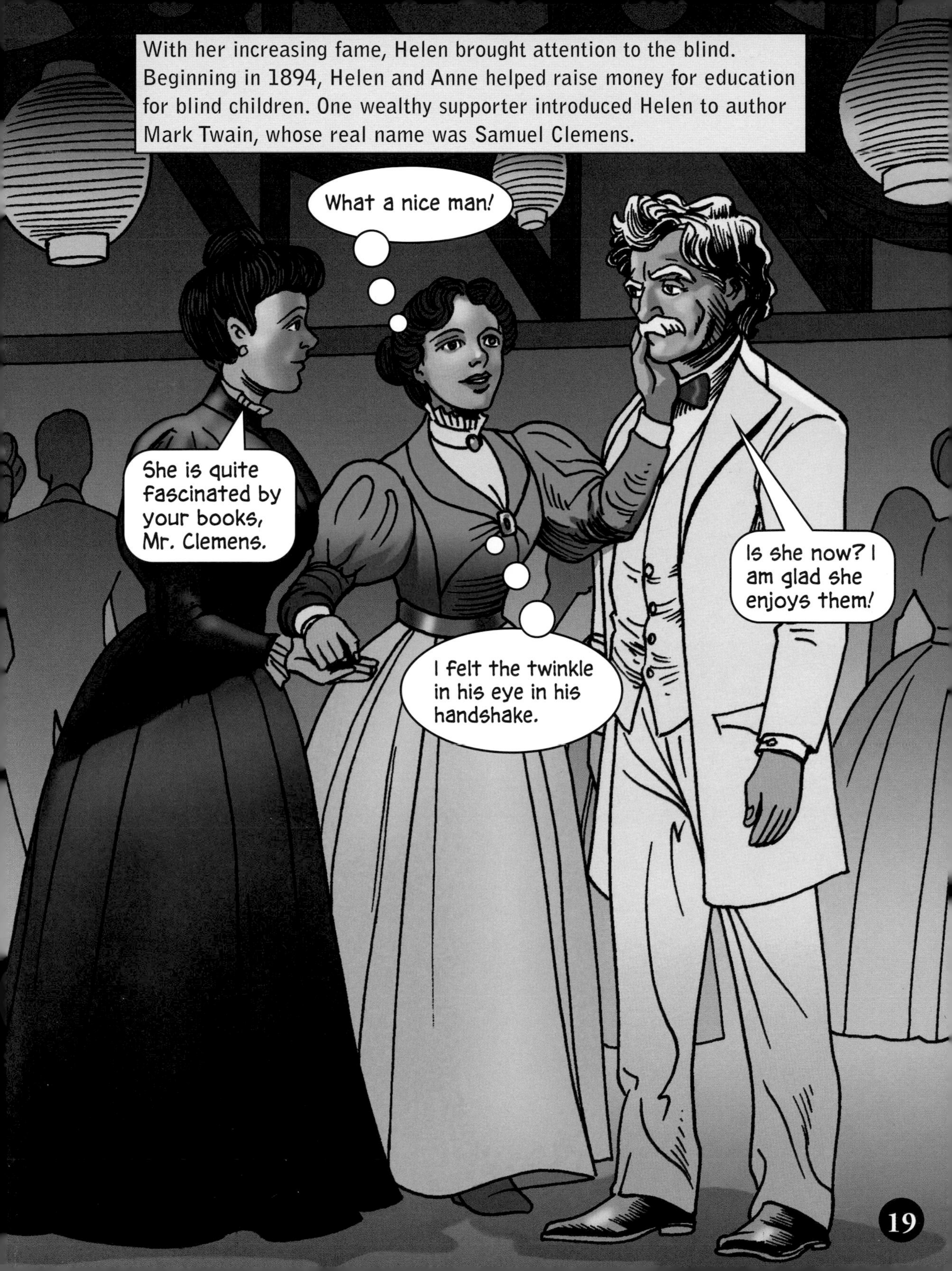
With her increasing fame, Helen brought attention to the blind. Beginning in 1894, Helen and Anne helped raise money for education for blind children. One wealthy supporter introduced Helen to author Mark Twain, whose real name was Samuel Clemens.
What a nice man!
She is quite fascinated by your books, Mr. Clemens.
Is she now? I am glad she enjoys them!
I felt the twinkle in his eye in his handshake.

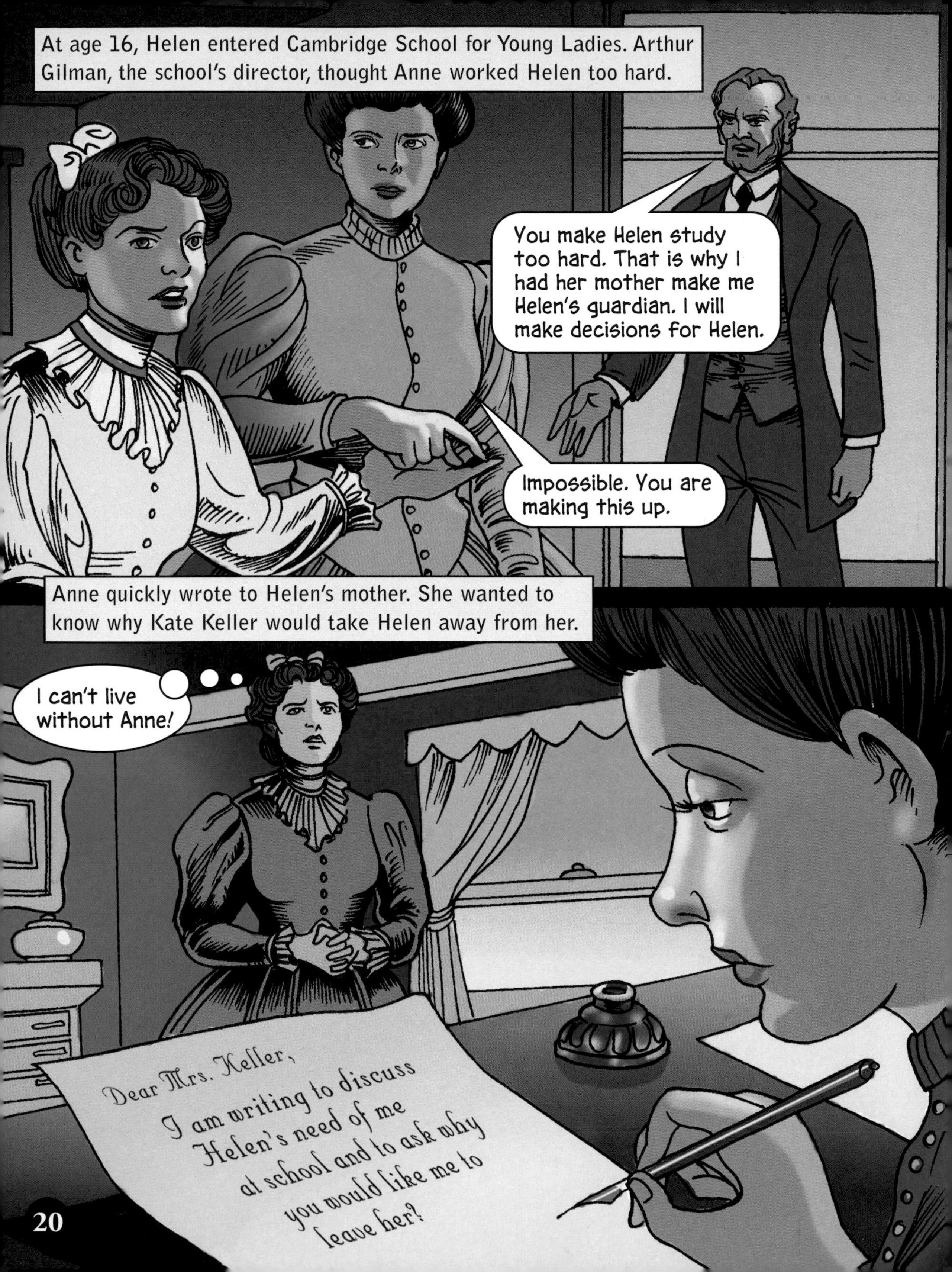
At age 16, Helen entered Cambridge School for Young Ladies. Arthur Gilman, the school's director, thought Anne worked Helen too hard.
You make Helen study too hard. That is why I had her mother make me Helen's guardian. I will make decisions for Helen.
Impossible. You are making this up.
Anne quickly wrote to Helen's mother. She wanted to know why Kate Keller would take Helen away from her.
I can't live without Anne!
Dear Mrs. Keller,
I am writing to discuss Helen's need of me at school and to ask why you would like me to leave her?

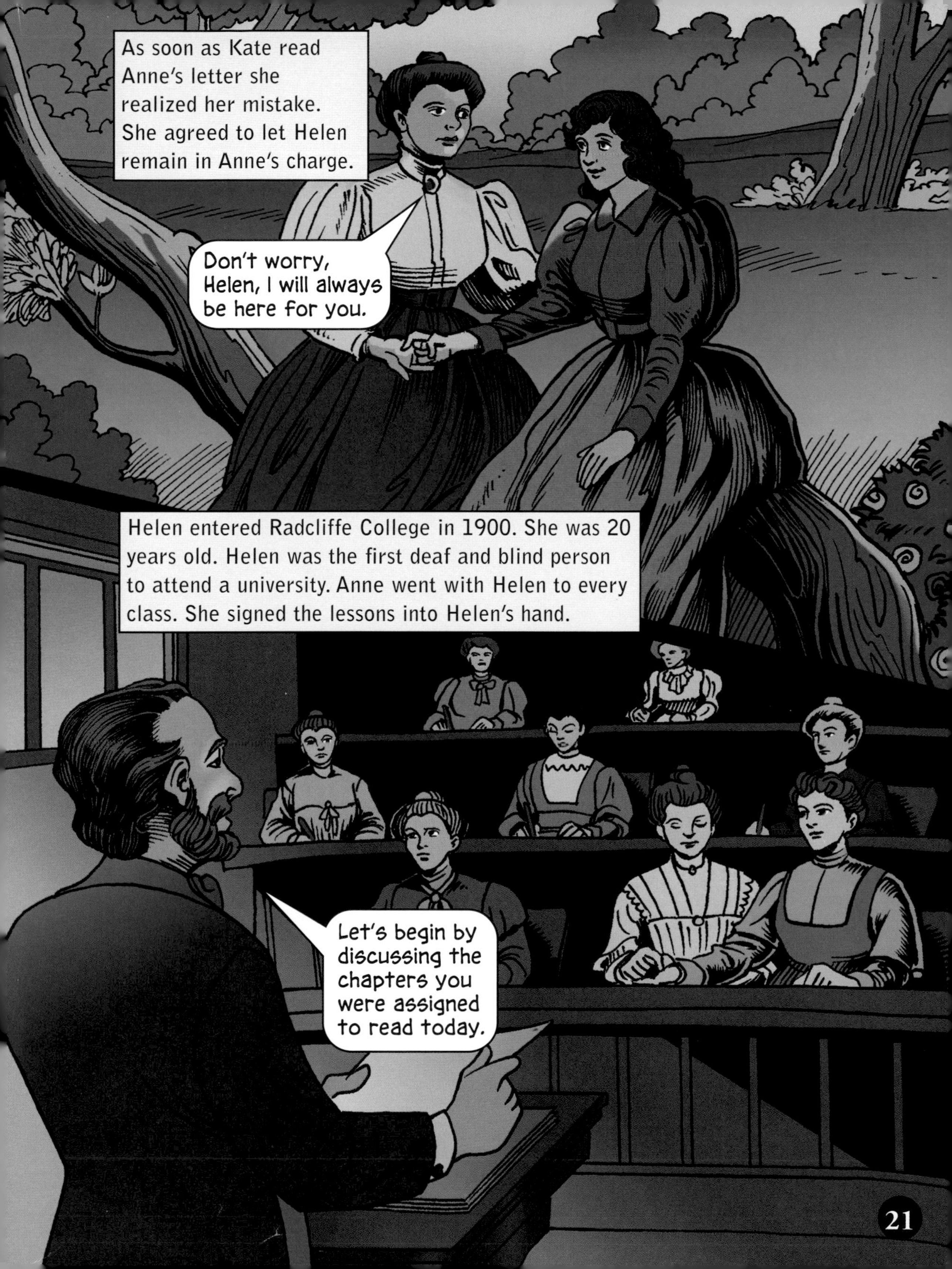
As soon as Kate read Anne's letter she realized her mistake. She agreed to let Helen remain in Anne's charge.
Don't worry, Helen, I will always be here for you.
Helen entered Radcliffe College in 1900. She was 20 years old. Helen was the first deaf and blind person to attend a university. Anne went with Helen to every class. She signed the lessons into Helen's hand.
Let's begin by discussing the chapters you were assigned to read today.

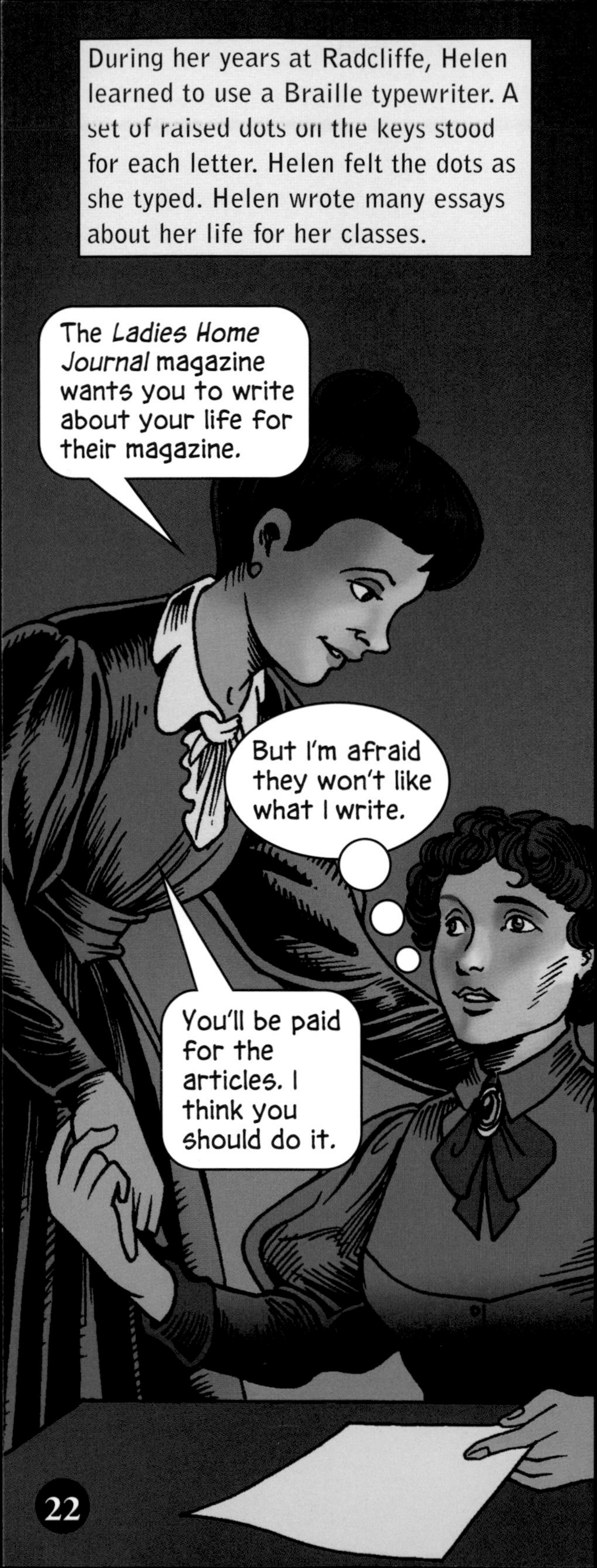
During her years at Radcliffe, Helen learned to use a Braille typewriter. A set of raised dots on the keys stood for each letter. Helen felt the dots as she typed. Helen wrote many essays about her life for her classes.
The *Ladies Home Journal* magazine wants you to write about your life for their magazine.
But I'm afraid they won't like what I write.
You'll be paid for the articles. I think you should do it.

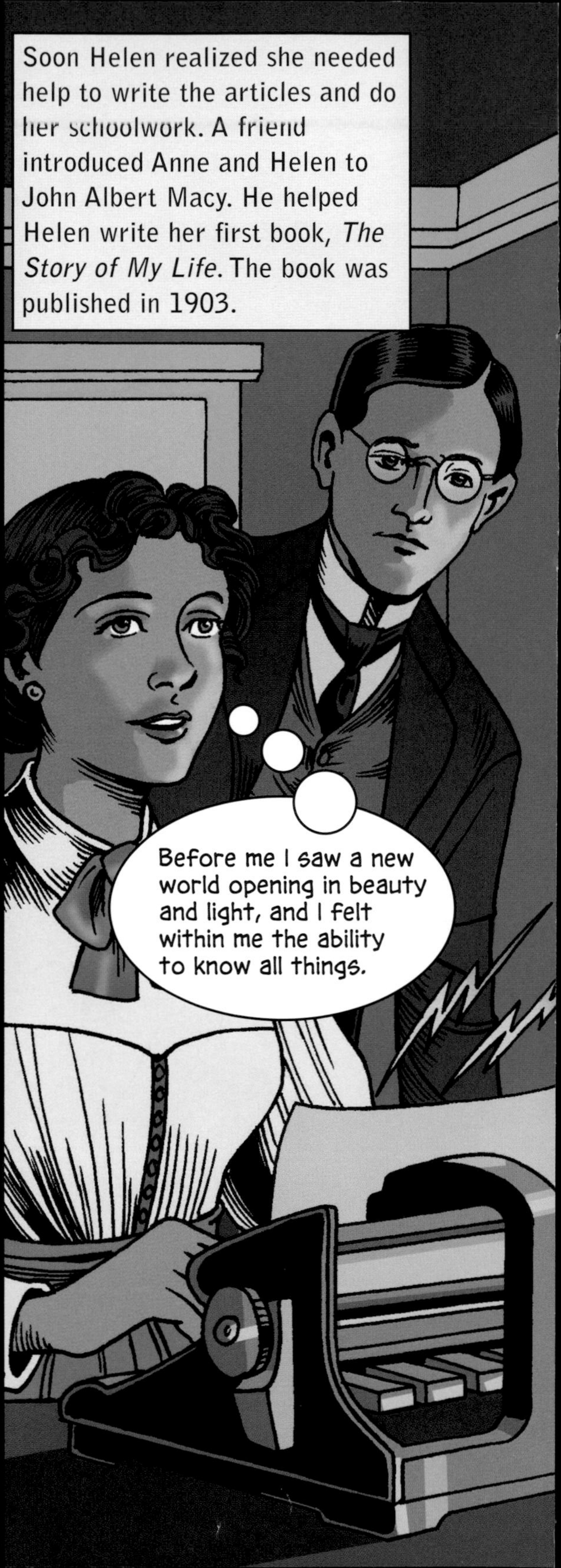
Soon Helen realized she needed help to write the articles and do her schoolwork. A friend introduced Anne and Helen to John Albert Macy. He helped Helen write her first book, *The Story of My Life*. The book was published in 1903.
Before me I saw a new world opening in beauty and light, and I felt within me the ability to know all things.

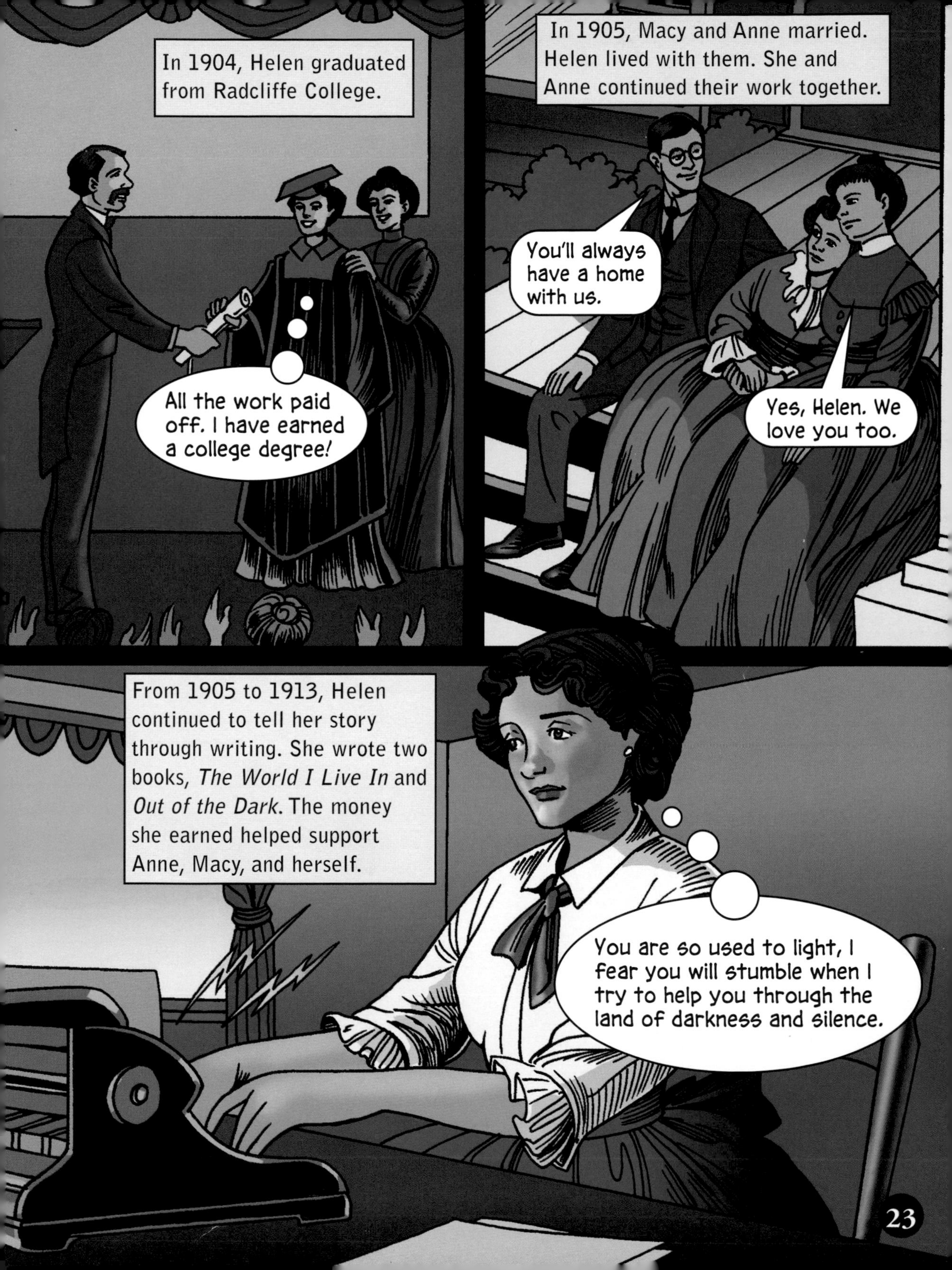
In 1904, Helen graduated from Radcliffe College.
All the work paid off. I have earned a college degree!
In 1905, Macy and Anne married. Helen lived with them. She and Anne continued their work together.
You'll always have a home with us.
Yes, Helen. We love you too.
From 1905 to 1913, Helen continued to tell her story through writing. She wrote two books, *The World I Live In* and *Out of the Dark*. The money she earned helped support Anne, Macy, and herself.
You are so used to light, I fear you will stumble when I try to help you through the land of darkness and silence.

CHAPTER 4

Working for Others

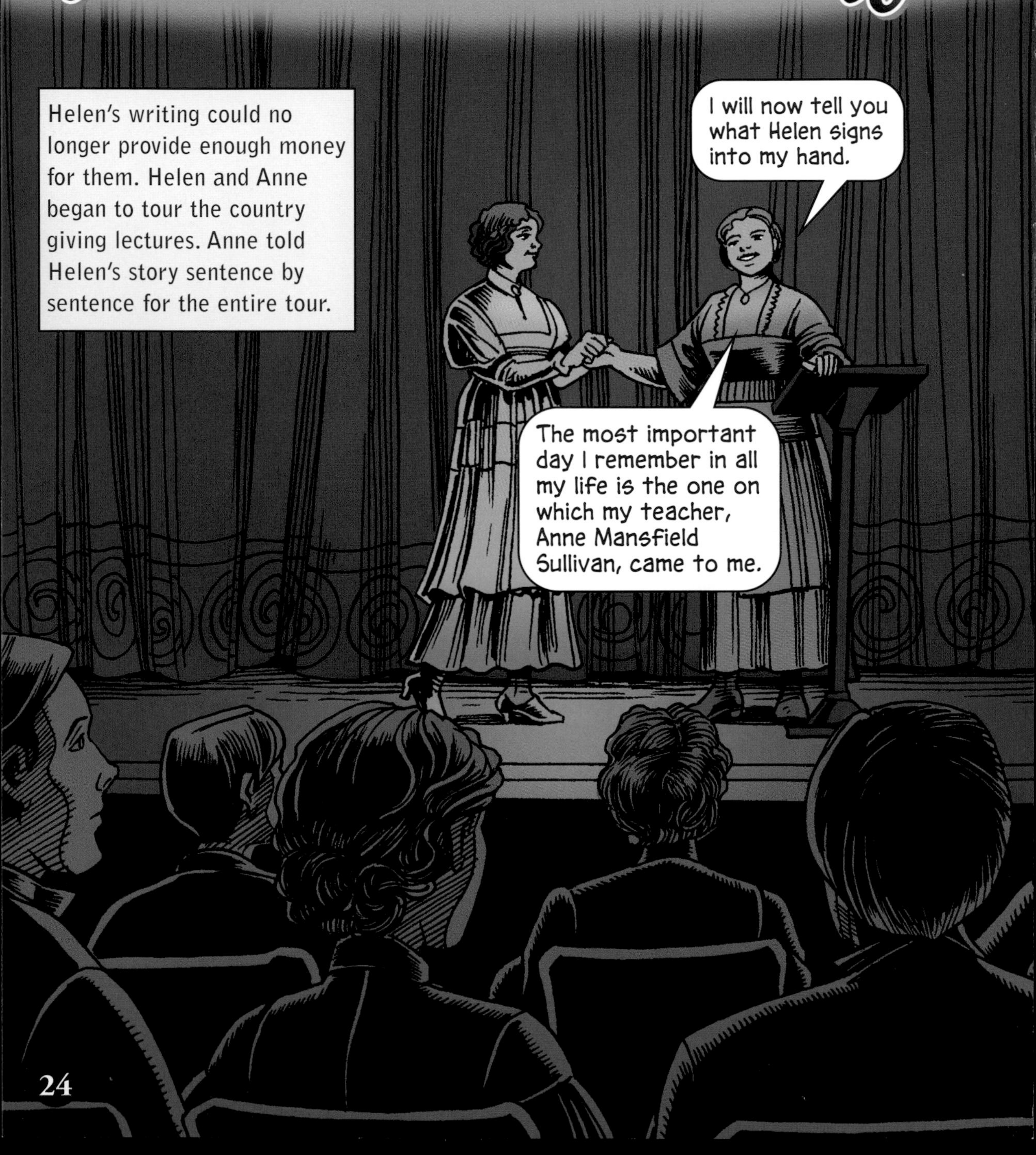
Helen's writing could no longer provide enough money for them. Helen and Anne began to tour the country giving lectures. Anne told Helen's story sentence by sentence for the entire tour.
I will now tell you what Helen signs into my hand.
The most important day I remember in all my life is the one on which my teacher, Anne Mansfield Sullivan, came to me.

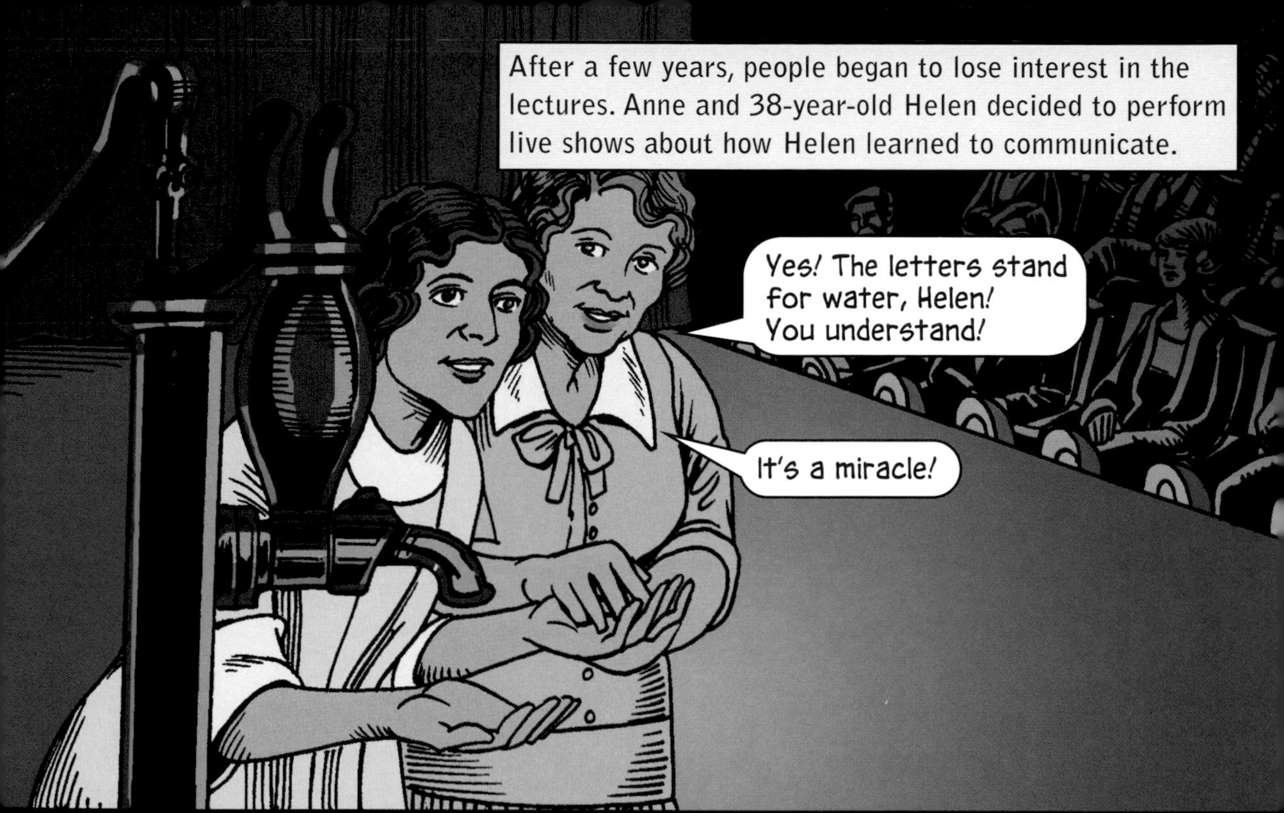
After a few years, people began to lose interest in the lectures. Anne and 38-year-old Helen decided to perform live shows about how Helen learned to communicate.
Yes! The letters stand for water, Helen! You understand!
It's a miracle!

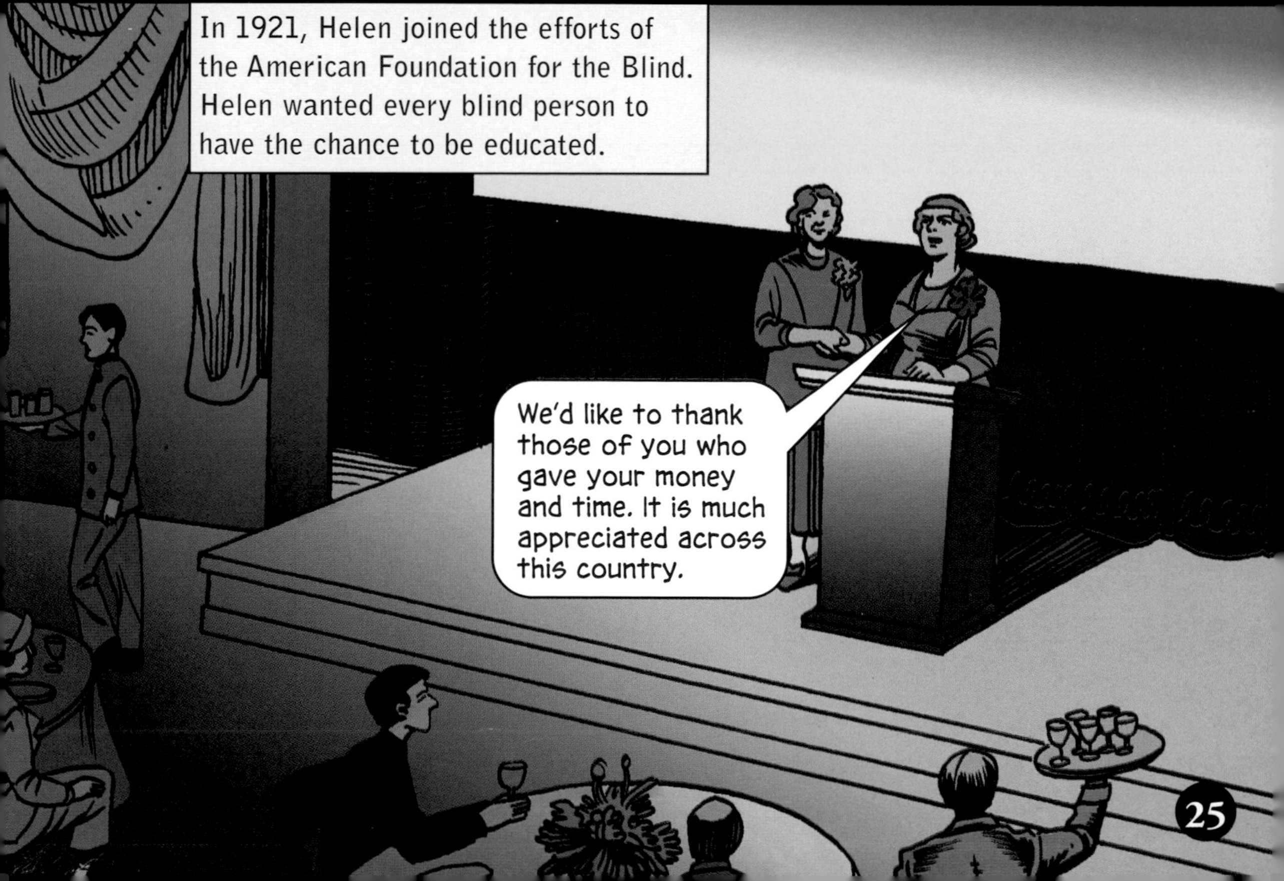
In 1921, Helen joined the efforts of the American Foundation for the Blind. Helen wanted every blind person to have the chance to be educated.
We'd like to thank those of you who gave your money and time. It is much appreciated across this country.

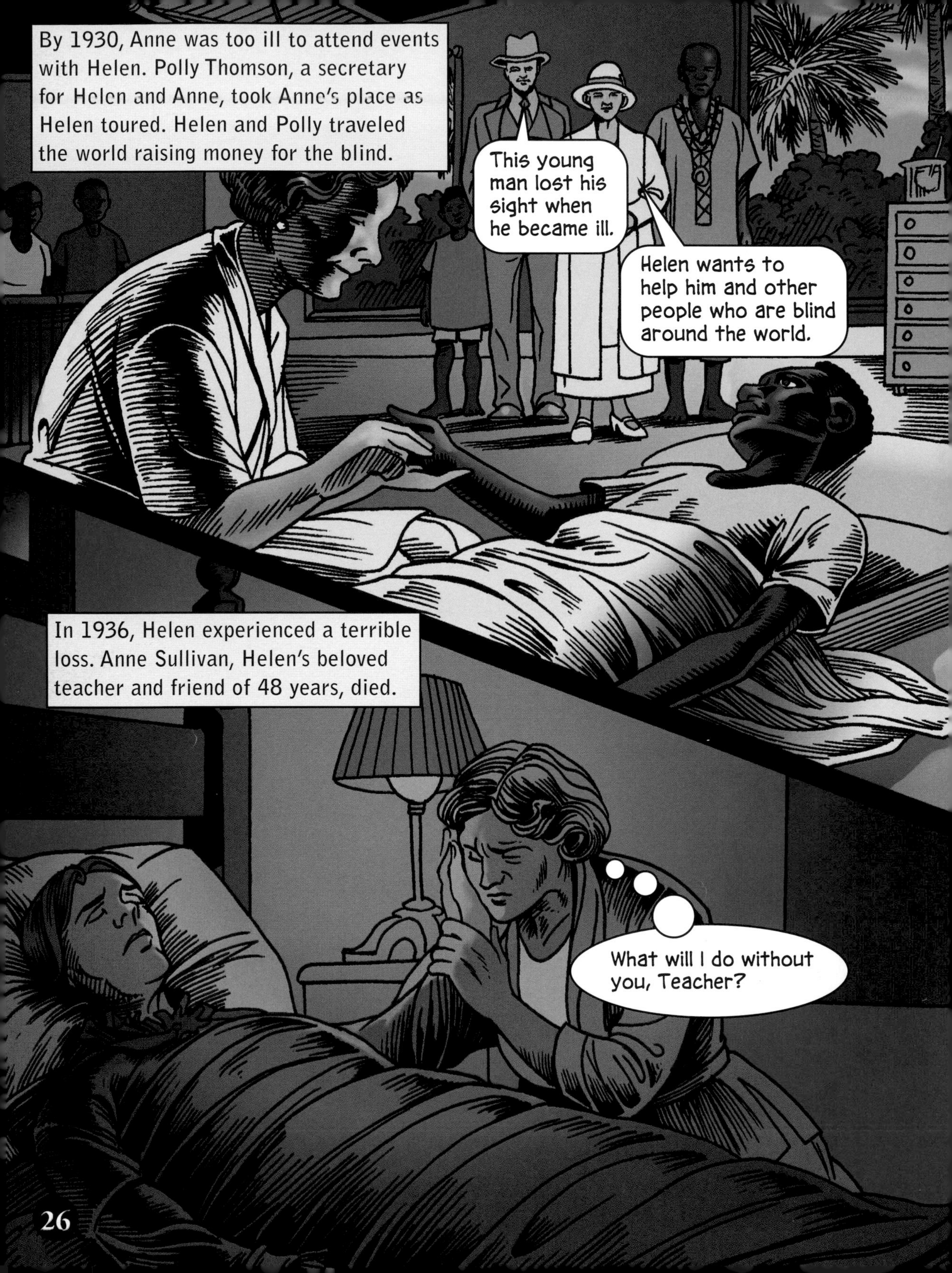
By 1930, Anne was too ill to attend events with Helen. Polly Thomson, a secretary for Helen and Anne, took Anne's place as Helen toured. Helen and Polly traveled the world raising money for the blind.
This young man lost his sight when he became ill.
Helen wants to help him and other people who are blind around the world.
In 1936, Helen experienced a terrible loss. Anne Sullivan, Helen's beloved teacher and friend of 48 years, died.
What will I do without you, Teacher?

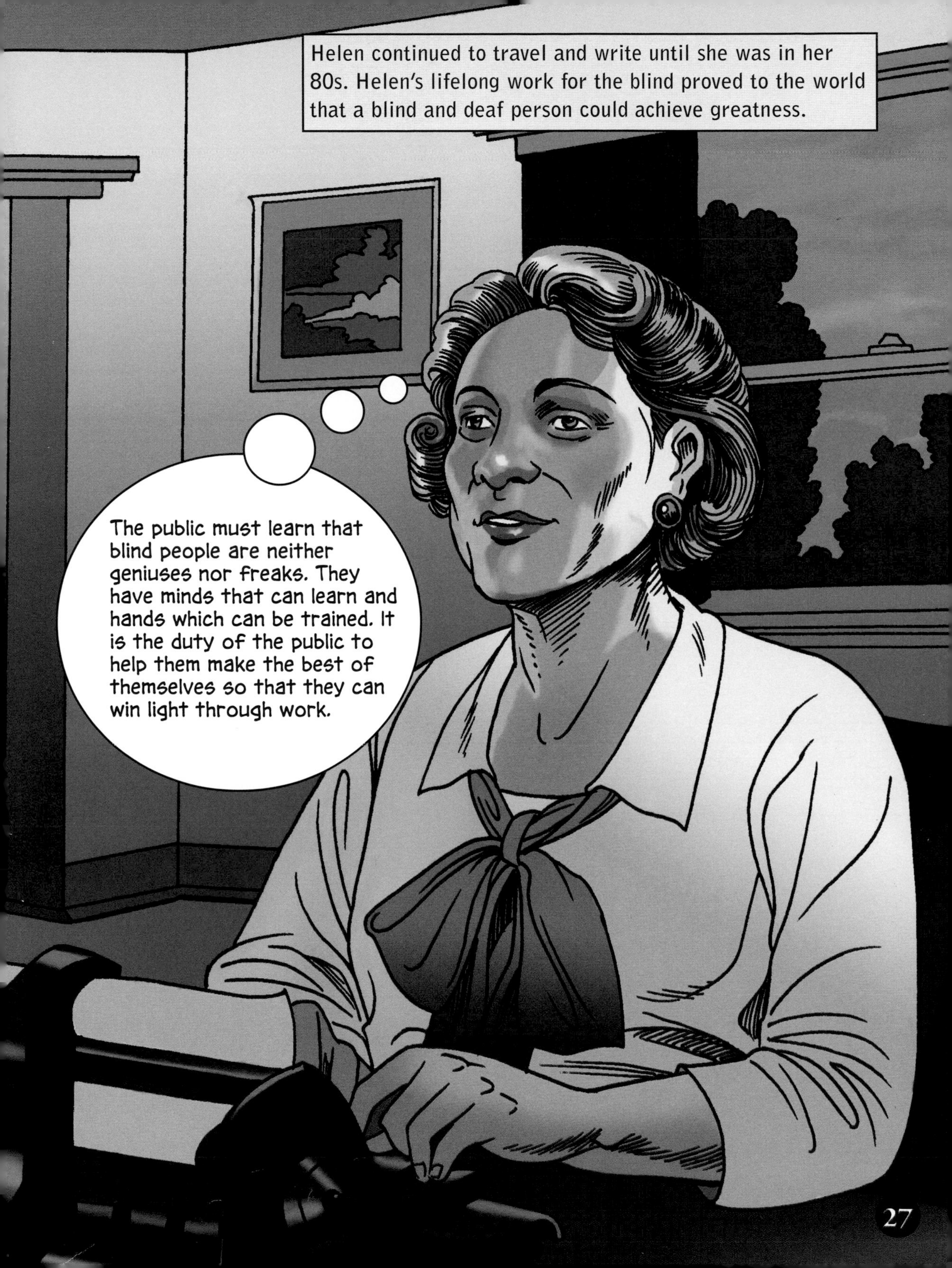
Helen continued to travel and write until she was in her 80s. Helen's lifelong work for the blind proved to the world that a blind and deaf person could achieve greatness.
The public must learn that blind people are neither geniuses nor freaks. They have minds that can learn and hands which can be trained. It is the duty of the public to help them make the best of themselves so that they can win light through work.

MORE ABOUT Helen Keller

✴ Helen Keller was born June 27, 1880, in Tuscumbia, Alabama. Her family's home was called Ivy Green because of the ivy that grew on the house.

✴ A high fever took Helen's sight and hearing in February 1882. Doctors today think the fever was caused by either meningitis or scarlet fever.

✴ Helen learned to swim, ride a bike, and ride a horse.

✴ Helen loved dogs. She always had at least one dog in her home.

✴ Helen tried to learn to speak, but she was never able to speak well enough for most people to understand her.

✴ People have made movies, performed Broadway plays, and written books about the life of Helen Keller.

- During their 48 years together, Helen and Anne rarely left each other's sides.
- Helen wrote 12 books during her life. *The Story of My Life* is her most popular book.
- The only continent Helen did not visit while raising money for the American Foundation for the Overseas Blind was Antarctica.
- All of Helen's work on her book *Teacher* was destroyed in a house fire. Helen eventually finished the book in 1955.
- Helen died peacefully in her sleep on June 1, 1968.
- The Braille plaque at the resting place of Helen and Anne in the Washington National Cathedral has already been replaced twice. People have touched the raised Braille dots so many times that the bumps wore away.

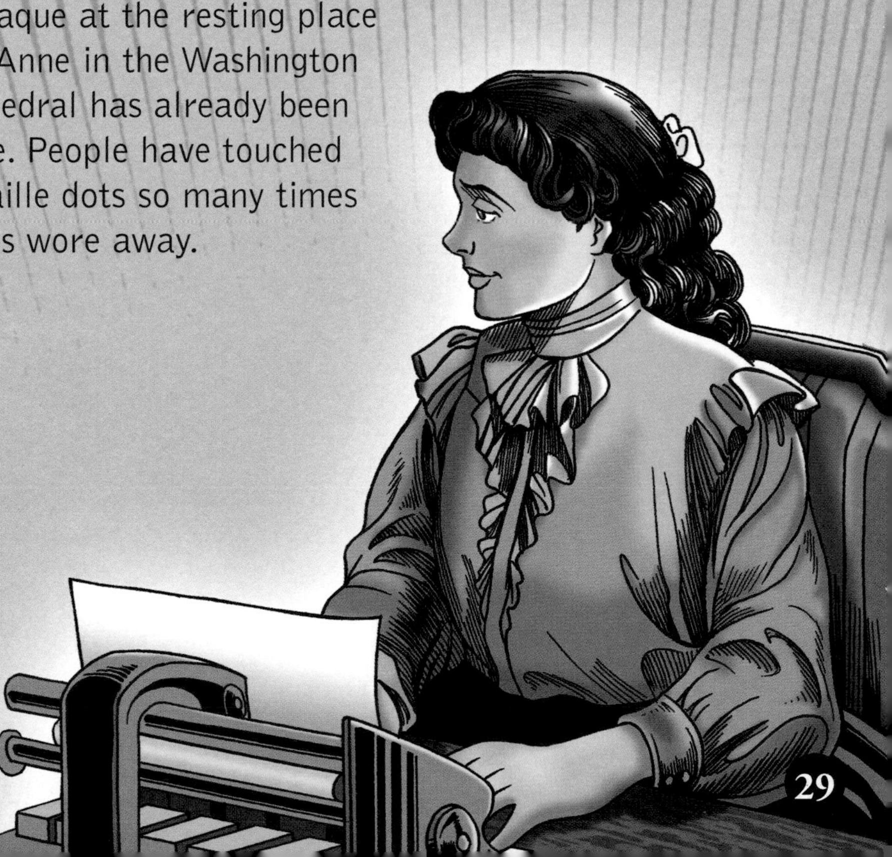

Glossary

Braille (BRAYL)—a set of raised dots that stand for letters and numbers; people use their fingertips to read the raised dots.

companion (kuhm-PAN-yuhn)—a person who spends time with another person

lecture (LEK-chur)—a talk given to a class or audience in order to teach something

orphan (OR-fuhn)—a child whose parents have died

plaque (PLAK)—a plate with words on it

Internet Sites

FactHound offers a safe, fun way to find Internet sites related to this book. All of the sites on FactHound have been researched by our staff.

Here's how:

1. Visit *www.facthound.com*
2. Type in this special code **0736849645** for age-appropriate sites. Or enter a search word related to this book for a more general search.
3. Click on the **Fetch It** button.

FactHound will fetch the best sites for you!

Read More

Adams, Colleen. *The Courage of Helen Keller.* The Rosen Publishing Group's Reading Room Collection. New York: Rosen, 2003.

DeVillier, Christy. *Helen Keller.* A Buddy Book. Edina, Minn.: Abdo, 2004.

Koestler-Grack, Rachel A. *The Story of Helen Keller.* Breakthrough Biographies. Philadelphia: Chelsea House, 2004.

Sutcliffe, Jane. *Helen Keller.* On My Own Biography. Minneapolis: Carolrhoda Books, 2002.

Bibliography

Braddy, Nella. *Anne Sullivan Macy: The Story Behind Helen Keller.* Garden City, New York: Doubleday/Doran, 1933.

Herrmann, Dorothy. *Helen Keller: A Life.* New York: A. Knopf, 1998.

Keller, Helen. *The Story of My Life.* New York: Doubleday, Page and Company, 1903.

Keller, Helen. *Teacher: Anne Sullivan Macy.* Garden City, New York: Doubleday and Company, 1955.

Index

American Foundation
  for the Blind, 25, 29
Anagnos, Michael, 8–9, 16,
  17

Bell, Alexander Graham, 6, 7,
  8, 14
Braille, 18, 22, 29
Bridgman, Laura, 7, 8

Cambridge School for Young
  Ladies, 20
Chisholm, Julian, 6
Clemens, Samuel. See Twain,
  Mark
Cleveland, President Grover,
  15

Gilman, Arthur, 20

Keller, Arthur (father), 4–9,
  16, 17
Keller, Helen,
  birth of, 28
  childhood of, 4–7,

death of, 29
education of, 11, 12, 14,
  16–18, 20–23
water pump, 12–13, 14, 25
writing books, 22–23, 24,
  29
Keller, Kate (mother), 4–9,
  11, 15, 16, 17, 20–21

Macy, John Albert, 22–23

Perkins Institution, 7, 8, 9,
  11, 15, 16, 17

Radcliffe College, 21, 22, 23

Sullivan, Anne, 8, 9, 10–13,
  15, 16–22, 23, 24–25, 26,
  29

Thomson, Polly, 26
Tuscumbia, Alabama, 6, 18,
  28
Twain, Mark, 18, 19